The International Pastor Experience

Compiled and Edited by Dr David Packer

DEDICATION

This is dedicated to all of the pastors of international churches abroad, but also to their wives, their families, their staff members, as well as to every member who has ever attended or served in these dynamic and strategic churches. This is a great work of God in this world today that is worthy of our support and encouragement

CONTENTS

BAC

Michael crane
visiting professor
2019 - 2020

ACKNOWLEDGMENTS

This work is a compilation and I am appreciative of all those who helped in different ways. The authors of each chapter have taken their time and energy to help pastors and churches around the world. But also others have encouraged the writing of this book. Scott Carter helped by introducing me to Michael Crane and Jacob Bloemberg. Jimmy Martin's enthusiasm for the book was also encouraging – he was the first to complete and submit his chapter. Larry Jones' encouragement and the help of the International Baptist Church Ministries in publishing copies of this book is also appreciated. The common goal in writing, contributing, and editing this book is to help the church of Jesus Christ through giving practical and helpful advice about international churches overseas. We believe the international church is a strategic work that God is doing, and we are blessed to be called to share in it. And if you have purchased this book and taken time to read it, then we are also appreciative of you for helping us fulfill our God-given calling and mission.

David Packer

Stuttgart, Germany

CHAPTER ONE
THE FUTURE OF INTERNATIONAL CHURCHES

By Dr Jimmy Martin
International Baptist Convention
General Secretary

Jimmy Martin lives in Frankfurt, Germany. He has been the General Secretary of the International Baptist Convention since 2003. Prior to that he served churches in his home state of Texas, USA, and was pastor of Faith Baptist Church in Kaiserslautern, Germany, from 1993 to 2003. He is a graduate of East Texas Baptist University and Southwestern Baptist Theological Seminary (MDiv and PhD). In his position as General Secretary he relates to international churches around the world. He and his wife Laurie have three married daughters and five grandchildren.

A funny thing happened on my way to lifelong ministry—I discovered the International Church! Although my wife, Laurie, and I considered and prayed about serving internationally when we were newly married, we could not point to a specific calling to leave our pastorate and move overseas to serve as church planters or whatever other assignment we might be given by a mission board.

We assumed that we would continue to serve God in the small Texas town where we lived, actively support missions as pray-ers and senders, and occasionally get involved in short-term mission trips as opportunities arose.

In 1992, we received encouragement to consider serving an English-language church in Germany associated with the European Baptist Convention. Largely due to my particular interest in Eastern Europe (the church had an active ongoing partnership in Romania), we decided we should at least look into this opportunity. Nine months later, we moved to Kaiserslautern, Germany, to serve as pastor of Faith Baptist Church, a largely US-military congregation. We were immediately confronted with both wonderful opportunities and significant challenges. I learned that many military members in the church were highly motivated disciples who were eager to serve and grow. It was a joy to serve such a church. At the same time, we were now living in two new cultures—the German culture and the military culture. We lived on the German economy, yet associated mostly with Americans who made up our church family. Angela, Leah, and Karis—our three daughters—were 9, 6, and 5 at the time. They immediately started German school and soon were speaking far better German than their parents. For ten years we were blessed to serve with these dear Christian people. It was like "pastoring a parade," with people staying an average of about three years before moving on to their next assignment.

In 2003, I accepted the call from the European Baptist Convention (and the Lord) to serve as its General Secretary. Although our roots as a group of churches were in planting and supporting US military congregations, the changing political landscape of Europe in the early 1990s brought closures of many US-military congregations and, at the same time, new opportunities to plant churches in Central and Eastern Europe. In cooperation with missionaries largely from the Southern Baptist Convention, the EBC had planted numerous international churches in key cities there—usually large cities with significant international English-speaking populations. These new English-language congregations typically included some of the following: international students, business people, diplomats, refugees, and nationals. The churches had members who were diverse in terms of race, culture, religious background, nationality, politics, and first language. The congregations were transient with two- to three-year typical assignments for most expat members.

In October of 2003, our family of churches changed its name to reflect the new realities—European Baptist Convention (EBC) became International Baptist Convention (IBC). We already had one church outside of Europe, with Emirates Baptist Church International in Dubai, UAE, having joined in 1997. We also were reaching internationals, not only US military members and their families.

Since that time, the IBC has continued to welcome churches from inside and outside Europe that feel a kinship with an organization that is reaching expats, the global diaspora. Currently we have churches in Europe, Asia, Africa, and the Americas with recent church plants in Panama City, Panama; Darmstadt, Germany; and Rome, Italy. We are not a large family of churches, but we are widely scattered. We are struggling with new challenges of seeking to involve and mobilize the current churches that make up our membership and at the same time to plant new churches. Our mission statement reflects this challenge and opportunity: "We exist to mobilize and multiply disciple-making churches."

What is the future of English-speaking international churches? Will they continue to multiply? Who will they reach, and how? What does an effective international church look like? What kinds of church planters and pastors will serve most effectively? What are the opportunities and challenges?

Opportunities

Recent feasibility studies in Latin America and various parts of Europe have convinced us that there is a great opportunity to reach expats. In addition to a few areas where a largely US-military congregation should be planted, there are numerous areas where international congregations could thrive. We are finding encouragement from local and English-speaking international pastors already serving in cities we have surveyed. "The harvest is plentiful but the laborers are few" is the message we are hearing.

Evangelization and Witness. Numerous studies have been made and reports written on the effects of globalization in our world and the impact this is having. In the past 30 years, the movement of people has become, according to T.V. Thomas, a "global phenomenon."[1] Reliable estimates place the number of expatriates ("global nomads"), people living outside their country of birth, at more than 200 million, more than 3% of the world population. For evangelicals, who see the openness of expats as a doorway for the Gospel, international churches can reach these people. As Thomas says, "Both the Great Commission mandate in Matthew 28:19-20, 'make disciples of all nations,' and Christ's divine exhortation, 'You are my witnesses' (Acts 1:8), demand that we evangelize the people on the move."

Graham Chipps, an international pastor for many years in Phnom Penh, Cambodia, writes, "Before much longer the majority of churches will be international or multicultural.... The international church with its multicultural and multinational character, and with its location in the crossroad cities of the world, is already on the front line."[2]

---

[1] T.V. Thomas, "Moving Ahead with God," a paper presented for the Global Diaspora Network, October 20, 2010.

[2] Graham Chipps, "A Future World and a Future Conference, posted on 11/29/14 in "Articles,"

International churches will not reach all global nomads. National churches will reach some. But many others, for a variety of reasons, are better reached through international churches, especially those speaking English, the *lingua franca* of much of the world. Together, the global church can join in evangelization, which the Lausanne Covenant defines as "The whole Church taking the whole gospel to the whole world." (The Lausanne Covenant was adopted in Lausanne, Switzerland, in 1974 at the International Congress on World Evangelization. Evangelical leaders, Billy Graham and John Stott, were leaders in the Lausanne Movement. For the full document, see http://www.lausanne.org/content/covenant/lausanne-covenant.)

International churches have the potential for significant evangelistic effectiveness. In the cities where they are located, international churches are finding members of unreached people groups (UPGs), people groups where evangelical Christians comprise less than 2% of the total population, and unengaged unreached people groups (UUPGs), UPGs where there is no church planting strategy underway. These people groups are much more open to the Gospel when they are refugees, students, members of a diplomatic corps, or business people living abroad. Many come from countries where the opportunity to hear the Gospel is very low and responding to the Gospel can be life threatening. Yet they are curious to hear more about Christianity. They are interested to learn English or improve their English language skills. When an international church reaches out to them to minister to their needs, barriers are broken down and they listen to the Gospel message. Some return to their countries of origin as disciples of Jesus and His witnesses.

I have heard numerous stories of expats coming to Christ in this way,

---

and I have personally known enough of these situations that I am convinced it is one of the greatest opportunities of the international church. For example, a father and two sons fled Iran as political refugees and came to Europe. They received practical help from an IBC church, heard the Gospel message, and responded. They were discipled and eventually left this European country for another, then another, and another. In each country, they led numerous Farsi-speakers to Christ, establishing churches and networks wherever they went. They maintain relationship and accountability with the international church where they first heard the Gospel.

International churches can be effective witnesses to global business people and their families who live in major cities of the world for two to three years. Most global postings by international businesses require long hours and significant travel. Families are often lonely and eager to connect with others in similar circumstances. A caring international church can offer such care and open the door for an evangelistic witness. A friend of mine, Paul, first heard the Gospel while attending an Alpha course sponsored by an international church. He began attending services in the church. He and his family are now active in the church where Paul serves as an elder.

Students studying internationally are often very open to hearing the Gospel when it is presented in a clear and loving way. One IBC pastor also serves as a student worker in several universities in his city. He has numerous opportunities to share the Gospel and to see students grow in an evangelical English-speaking church. Many of these students will return to their countries of origin as highly educated ambassadors for Christ.

Although the number of mostly military congregations in our family of churches has decreased, the ones that remain are among the largest and most effective in evangelistic zeal. The number of military members who enter Christian ministry as a second career is astounding. Many of these military members heard the Gospel while serving abroad. They were given the opportunity to serve and lead in an international church. Their families were discipled in an international church. They discovered the joy of multicultural mission through an international church.

International churches have as their focus reaching expats, but most also have members who are nationals. Reasons for this include a desire to improve English-language skills, having a spouse whose preferred language is English, being invited by a colleague at work, having a history of living internationally, or having no interest in attending a national church but being curious about faith and seeing the international church as interesting and a cultural learning experience. For whatever reason they discover Christ-followers serious about their faith, hear the Gospel, and find a home in an international church. Some of them eventually return to a church in their native language due to the preference of children studying in the national schools, but they remain grateful for the opportunity to have started their walk with Christ in an international church.

Government workers from around the world often hear the Gospel through the witness of international churches. One IBC church regularly has officials from the Chinese government attending worship services. Another IBC church has an effective ministry with diplomats through its English-language courses. Several of our churches regularly conduct Bible studies at United Nations offices. International churches are uniquely poised to reach decision-makers from around the world.

International churches have a unique opportunity to live out the reconciling power of the Gospel of Jesus Christ that they preach. Bruce Milne, who served an international church in Vancouver, Canada, for seventeen years, calls the international church a "new-humanity" church (Eph. 2:15). This "new-humanity" church is learning what the first-century church learned, to practice a "radically new quality of communal life in which natural diversities of ethnicity, race and every other major human diversity were overcome in a way that astonished, fascinated and finally won a multitude of followers from the watching world around them."[3] The "new-humanity" church can bear strong witness to a world where differences often define and divide people. The international church is "a powerful demonstration in today's world of God's age-long purpose to 'bring all things in heaven and on earth together under one head, even Christ' (Eph. 1:10)."[4]

Global Mission. International churches are uniquely poised for global mission. There are numerous opportunities to link up with other "Great Commission" groups who are serving where the international church is located, often in the same city. Many international churches offer logistical and personal support to churches, humanitarian teams, and others who would like to meet human needs in places around the world. In addition, there are opportunities to do effective evangelism, social ministry, and relief projects of their own as they serve alongside national churches and beyond. Leaders make a wise investment when they involve their members in mission. It is often the case that God touches the hearts of people doing mission on a short-term basis, and they continue in this ministry long-term.

Challenges

The idea of leading an international "multi-everything" church has a great appeal for many. In practice, it is hard work and is not for every leader. What has the potential for being the strongest witness

---

[3] Bruce Milne, *Dynamic Diversity: Bridging Class, Age, Race and Gender in the Church*, Downer's Grove, IL: InterVarsity Press, 2007, p. 10.

[4] Milne, p. 14.

to the reconciling power of Christ to bring people together—the congregation itself—can also be disastrous. Here are some of the greatest challenges that international churches face.

Conflict arising out of diversity. Managing and leveraging diversity is a significant challenge in the international church. The Apostle Paul's command to the church in Ephesus to "make every effort to keep the unity of the Spirit though the bond of peace" (NIV, Eph. 4:3) is needed advice. Bruce Milne notes some of the diversities that must be transcended: "gender, generation, ethnicity, race, color, family unit, social and economic status, educational opportunity, mental and physical healthy, spiritual history, spiritual gifting and personality type."[5] Although all churches must deal with some of these issues, international churches must manage them to a greater degree. I have seen churches divide over the usual challenges such as pastoral authority, worship styles, understanding of church organization, theology, and the practice of charismatic gifts. I have also seen international churches in conflict due to tribal differences among members from the same country and polygamous marriages in the church.

Leadership. Pastor David Packer describes clearly the challenge of leading an international church: "Often the very fabric of the church is tested and strained as people who come into the church have different cultural expectations and definitions of leadership and fellowship, as well as worship and church financial budgeting. Christ is not divided, but centuries of cultural separations from one another are not easy to overcome. And many of these differences ambush us..."[6]

Transience. The challenge of continuity in churches where people are constantly coming and going is very real. Having served in such

---

[5] Milne, p. 14.
[6] David Packer, *Look Who God Let into the Church: Understanding the Nature and Sharpening the Impact of a Multicultural Church,* David Packer, 2013, p. 7.

an environment for more than twenty years now, I often remind new pastors to take a breath, trust God, and have faith that God will bring new people to replace those who will be leaving, especially during transitional times of the year. Keep doing what the church is called to do—"make disciples"—and know that God will take care of His church.

Darryl Evetts, an IBC church planter and leader, identifies three processes involved in disciple making in a local church: assimilation, transformation, and mobilization. He describes some of the challenges involved in transient churches: emotional toll of people continually leaving the churches, scheduling activities and programming events, continually rebuilding or restarting ministries, and the constant need to recruit and develop volunteers and leaders.[7]

The Future International Church

I believe in international churches. International churches, with all their diversity, reflect the redemption and reconciliation purposes of God in a beautiful way, and thus are a powerful witness to the truth of the Gospel. I believe there is a bright future for the international Church but not necessarily for all international churches. I have seen international churches that seem to grow at a steady pace, pursuing the future with optimism inspired by the Holy Spirit, and managing conflict and other challenges in a healthy way. I have seen other international churches that seem to have a culture of unhealthy conflict or shortsighted vision that keeps them from growing consistently in a healthy way. The future is bright for international churches that are characterized by some or all of the following qualities, which must be a part of the DNA of the leadership.

---

[7] Darryl Evetts, *Making Disciples in Transient Communities: a Thesis Project Report Submitted in Partial Fulfillment of the Requirements for the Doctor of Ministry Degree in Global and Contextual Leadership, St. Paul, MN: Bethel Seminary, 2014, pp. 8-9, 119.*

Mission. International churches and their leaders must be convinced of the necessity of taking the Gospel to the whole world and of "making disciples of all nations." The international church is not called to be merely a "home away from home" for expatriates but a global worshiping, ministering, witnessing, discipling, and sending body for people. The church and its leaders must be convinced that they are called to serve the global community where they are located and beyond.

Vision. International churches and their leaders must be able to picture the future God has for them. They must refuse to get stuck in the past or the present, but rather they must dream together of how they can serve God's purposes for them in the future. They must not allow prejudice or parochial ideas about how a church should function to cripple the creative diversity that God has given them. Visionary leaders who are also strategic thinkers will see their church as a base for mission expansion and will guide the church to form strategies that reach people locally and globally.

Core Values. Central to the international church's future will be the values that drive their decisions and ministries. In addition to core values such as biblical instruction, prayer, community, worship, and evangelism, the international church must magnify these values to an international, multicultural level. This means such things as global evangelism, prayer for the nations of the world, diversity as a gift to be celebrated, relationship building in the midst of transience, and discipleship defined in terms of developing "world Christians" whose life directions have been solidly transformed by a world vision. (See the excellent article on what a "world Christian" is by David Bryant, "To Be a World Christian," taken from his book, *In the Gap*, 1979, and printed on The Traveling Team website— www.thetraveliingteam.org).

Relationships. It is not possible to practice biblical Christianity apart from healthy relationship building. International church members often express how they have been stretched through friendships with people from many cultures and races, and how it has helped them in their growth as Christ-followers. It is a challenge to provide opportunities and structures in the church that encourage deeper and broader relationships, but it is essential for a healthy international church. "The new-humanity model offers a way of doing church that is profoundly rooted in the Scriptures, and so has divine authorization. It is massively relevant to our times.... It is profoundly missional and growth-oriented.... [It] represents a way forward for the evangelical faith in this time...."[8] Leaders who encourage and foster relationships among diverse people are responding to the hopes and desires of people now and in the future.

Calling and Development of Leaders. The church rises and falls on its leadership. A leader, for good or bad, makes a world of difference. For this reason, international churches need to be very careful and deliberate as they seek to call a pastor and set apart other leaders. They also need to be intentional in developing effective leaders. The development of effective leaders must be a priority for transient churches where the pool of leaders is constantly in need of replenishing.

All churches need effective leaders who can lead the church ahead toward its God-given mission. International churches should intentionally seek to call and develop leaders who will lead spiritually out of a personal and consistent walk with the Lord that is produced by fervent prayer and biblical conviction. Effective spiritual leaders will lead with a humble spirit that chooses to listen and learn from fellow followers of Christ in mutual commitment and accountability. Leaders who possess a robust and global theology that is Christ-centered with a strong biblical base and gospel focus

---

[8] Milne, p. 173.

will be better prepared to keep the church on track as far as beliefs and practices that are essential, non-essential, and harmful. Leaders who will take the time and effort to increase their own emotional intelligence so that they grow both in self-awareness and social awareness—knowing their own strengths and weakness as well as those of the people they lead—will work more effectively with others on the leadership team and with members whose views might be very different from their own.

Leaders who have a genuine love for internationals and a heart to reach internationals will be better equipped to grow congregations that understand and appreciate one another and to reach out to others in kind and compassionate ways with the Gospel. Leaders who are equipped with peacemaking skills will be more effective in building a culture of grace and health in churches where differing perspectives, experiences, values, and ways of communicating can lead to harmful conflict. Leaders who have gifts and capacities for flexibility and creativity will be less inclined to try to create churches like the places where they came from and more inclined to discover the uniqueness of each local family of God. Leaders who are willing to minister alongside others, who see "cooperation" and "partnership" in a positive light, and see the Body of Christ as interdependent will be able to lead churches that see themselves not as independent from others but rather totally dependent on God and mutually dependent on others.

In Conclusion

I believe that international, multicultural churches ARE the church of the future. The realities of increased globalization, diversification, multiculturalism, and transience all point to a future that is ripe for a "new-humanity" church that can offer the hope, truth, and love found in Christ alone. The gospel is Good News for all people everywhere, all cultures and all nations. The local church is the "tip of the spear" to bring the Gospel to the world. The local church has been called "God's shopping window" to the world, and the international church offers a bright hope to see God's reconciling, redeeming message lived out by His people.

CHAPTER TWO
A THIRD CULTURE KID EXPERIENCE AS PASTOR
OF AN INTERNATIONAL CHURCH

By David Fresch
Senior Pastor
North Sea Baptist Church
Stavanger, Norway

David has served as Senior Pastor of North Sea Baptist Church, Stavanger, Norway, since 2009. Through his mission organization, "Fresch Ministries International" he helps develop church leaders around the world. He and his wife Scottie have two daughters, Lily and Ellie.

"I was never any good at languages, so I thought there was no place for me on the mission field, but if I had known about English-speaking international churches when I was younger, I would have applied to pastor one."

Pastor Bill Ankerberg made the above comment to me over lunch one Sunday after interviewing me at his church in southern California. His goal was to raise awareness with his congregation about what God is doing around the world through international churches.

English-speaking international churches provide an amazing

opportunity for the spread of the Gospel and the equipping of the saints. In our churches people from all over the world, from every walk of life, and from every denominational background, gather to worship God and fellowship with the saints. Sunday mornings are to me a picture of what heaven will look like. And even though you do not have to learn a new language to pastor one, you do have to learn a new culture.

Unlike Bill, I have had the opportunity to know and be involved in international churches since my earliest memories, having been raised by a father who is in the oil industry and first moving abroad at the age of three and joining an International Baptist Church in the Netherlands. The following year we moved to Norway, where we joined North Sea Baptist Church, the church I now pastor.

I first moved to Norway at the age of four, and my family quickly got involved at North Sea. We found the church to be unlike any church we had ever been at or would ever be at again. The sense of family and unity at the church was beyond anything we had ever experienced. It seemed that since basically everyone at the church was transient, having moved to Norway for a job that would only keep them there for two to five years, they understood how hard it could be to move to Norway and be so far from home. So they became a family, brothers and sisters in Christ, spending not just Sundays together but taking family retreats as a church family, members going on vacation together, and being there for one another when babies were born or when difficulties struck.

My family left Stavanger when I was nine and move back to Oklahoma and soon after to Texas, but I had a love for Norway and for North Sea Baptist that would not fade away, and I had become a third culture kid.

I felt a call to ministry in middle school, and years later, after working at two churches in the US and a Christian drug recovery program, I was called to return to Norway with my wife and our oldest daughter (our second daughter was born in Norway a year

18

later), and we began a journey that has had its ups and downs but been incredibly exciting. I first worked as the associate pastor here at North Sea and then, for the majority of my nine years here, as the Senior Pastor. Over the years, certain aspects of ministering in a third-culture setting have become apparent to me, which I would like to share with you.

A DIFFERENT KIND OF COMMUNITY

Our church, like most international churches, is made up of people from many different nations and denominational backgrounds. This makes for a vibrant, but sometimes difficult, community. It is vibrant, because so many cultures are coming together. When you have a potluck, dishes may be brought that you do not recognize! Songs that people request for worship may be quite literally foreign to you. People in the church may come to you with mission requests to help out with a need in their home country, something close to their heart, even though it may be thousands of miles away from your church or your own home country. These and other symptoms of an international church make for an exciting ministry, but the challenges are equally diverse.

People from different cultures may have vastly different experiences with church and pastors. Some will not expect you to interact with them at all, being shocked when you invite them to your house, while others may expect to meet with you weekly, even though they are not looking for any counseling or discipling in their lives. Some church goers will want different styles of music and have different levels of comfort with charismatic expressions during worship. Almost all will reveal to some extent that "this is not how we did things at my church back home", which can be one of the most wearing complaints to deal with repeatedly. Usually it is stated more like this, "Well, at MY church back home...", as they seek to explain to you how it should be done at this church now.

I believe the best approach to the pros and cons is to embrace the international church for what it is, leveraging its strengths for

Kingdom advancement.

FOSTERING CULTURE

The first step in this process, according to my experience, is to spend time fostering a culture of unity. Here at North Sea, our slogan is "United in Love, Encouraged in Heart, Equipped for Impact". Now I want to be clear, our goal is not to simply have a loving, inward looking community. Our goal is to make disciples, and often, as we say here, "send out missionaries on Exxon's payroll." We want all of our people, no matter who they work for, to see themselves as missionaries as they are sent around the world. We want them to be mindful of the impact they can have as God, not their company, ordains for them to move from place to place. That is our eventual goal for our people, but the first step in this process is fostering a culture of love.

Seeing as our people come from all over the world, uniformity is not an option at North Sea, nor would we want it to be. But unity is not only an option, but a necessity – unity in the midst of great differences. I often quote John 13:35: "By this everyone will know that you are my disciples, if you love one another."

This may sound simple, but in an international church there are cultural differences and prejudices that can sometimes pose quite a barrier to unity. If we cannot live as the family of God inside the church, then we are not ready to offer anything to those outside the church.

I have found in churches that there is a level of "trickle-down culture", where the culture found in the leadership drips down the ranks ultimately all the way to the visitor on a Sunday morning. In churches where leadership lacked unity and love, the other members could feel it, and I have even witnessed members taking sides (akin to I follow Apollos and you follow Paul).

So I begin by developing a culture of love and trust with the leaders. It may sound odd to say, "I begin", when I have been here nearly nine years as of writing this chapter, but with the transient nature of most international churches, a pastor may feel like he is beginning all over again every fall after the annual summer transition. To develop a culture of love and trust, I develop true friendships with the leaders. I do this by taking them to lunch, having their families over, starting every fall with a deacons dinner where we go out as a team but cannot talk about church business, have a leadership retreat every year that has both a "business" element as well as team building elements, and even host a dinner for leadership couples at my house.

Hopefully these initiatives develop true friendships and also show my leaders that I truly care about them; I am not simply looking to "use" them to help me get ministry done, but I am willing to invest myself into their lives. We do not always agree, even though we are friends, but we always remain united, and we put our relationships first before our ideas of how the church should run. So I believe we are fulfilling Jesus command to love one another and to put others before ourselves.

This love and unity in leadership, which in my church starts with the deacons, trickles down to the other leaders and eventually to the rest of the laity and even to the visitor. I have had countless visitors comment on the love they felt the first time they walked into North Sea, and that sense of familial love, shown even to an outsider, is something I greatly desire to preserve.

One thing that all of the congregants at North Sea do seem to have in common is an element of "international" in who they are. Even the Norwegians who attend NSBC are international in some sense, either having been raised abroad or having married a foreigner. This common ground gives everyone a sense of not belonging in the indigenous culture here and creates a need for one another. Some have even said they no longer feel as comfortable in their "own" culture as they do being in an international culture. These people have become third culture themselves, but the third culture, when living in the international community in a place like Stavanger, becomes the first culture. Some people I know have actively chosen to stay in international assignments because the "international" culture they find in cities all over the world is the culture they have grown to relate to most closely.

But most of these people have no natural family in town besides their immediate family, and so, when love is evident in the church, the church is able to become their family, as I believe God intended. When a new baby is born, it is their church family that brings them meals. When illness strikes, it is their church family that offers to watch their children, so they can recover. When opportunities to travel for vacation arise, it is often members of their church family who are ready and willing to travel with them.

Encouraging and capitalizing on this sense of unity is a key to having a healthy international church. As a pastor, there are other ways that I have had to adapt to the international culture as well, even though I myself was a third culture kid.

PREACHING

I realized early on in my time here that the approach to ministry I had taken while in the US needed to be adjusted for international ministry. This first became clear to me in my preaching, because even though I fit in culturally, my sermons relied heavily on American examples and phrases. My wife, who is quite sensitive to such things, pointed this out to me, so I could adjust my preaching style.

While the Scriptures apply to all cultures, a good preacher needs to be able to communicate God's Word to the hearers in his church. I try to find examples to use in my sermons that highlight people from countries that are represented in our congregation. I also strive to be sensitive to the many backgrounds in our church. I come from an upper middle class family in the oil business, and I worked at two churches in the Houston area – an oil mecca, so I can tend to preach to those internationals most like me in the congregation and forget that we have refugees, immigrants, and workers from many other walks of life.

This also means, as in all churches, that people may be in very different places spiritually and emotionally. Looking out on a Sunday morning, I may see a refuge from a war-torn country who is missing his family and worried about their safety back home, while he is struggling to find a job and make ends meet in this foreign country he has found himself in with its unpleasant climate and unfamiliar foods. In the same service, a young oil professional may be sitting there in a state of ecstasy as her recent move to Norway is a sign of her rising star in the company she works for and financial freedom in years to come; she is excited about this new country she has found herself in, the possibility for winter sports, and the chance to travel around Europe on weekends. Preaching in a way that has a bearing on both their lives continues to be a challenge for me, making sure I consider both of them equally as I seek to share God's truth with them, comfort them, and challenge them.

SMALL GROUPS

Bible study done in small groups is an essential element of many churches. Running these in an international setting has some added challenges.

First, if the church runs Bible studies that simply go through Scripture, then there needs to be a leader, and with so many different Christian backgrounds in the church, it can be difficult to make sure the leader is in line with the doctrine of the local church. For us, the greatest concern we have is for our children, so those involved in teaching children have to sign a covenant that they will not teach nor promote doctrines that are contrary to the doctrines of NSBC.

If, on the other hand, the church chooses to use curriculum from an outside source, then you have the challenge of finding something that is not too "American" or any other culture, that may either feel irrelevant to an international group or insensitive.

Group discussions can also go places that I have not considered in the past. While in Texas, I never expected to have anyone speak out against democracy and claim that it was unbiblical to vote, but that is the sort of thing you may hear from Christians in an international setting. I am sure you could hear that in America too, but not in the types of churches I had been a part of, as they were rather uniform in the type of people in attendance from the color of the people to their politics, and North Sea is anything but uniform!

So realize that group discussions can be quite lively and go into unexpected territory. If there is a sense of love in the group, then this can be a very good thing. When we have different people making opposing cases from Scripture, it is an opportunity for everyone to dig more deeply into the Bible. Hopefully, people come out of it more rooted in Scripture and better able to identify truth. If the leader has built a good personal relationship with everyone in the group, then he or she should be able to restore unity, should a discussion get out of hand.

RELATIONSHIPS IN GENERAL

Speaking of politics, do not speak of politics. I mentioned the issue of democracy above, but overall, I avoid political discussions. First, the people most likely to want to discuss politics in my experience has been Americans, and many of the people in my church and attending small groups, are not Americans. Second, the views internationally can vary far more greatly than what we witness in the US where there seems to be only two sides to any issue. And because of America's standing in the world, many people in your church may have a view on America and her policies, even if they do not truly understand the politics involved. Therefore, it is not worth jeopardizing your influence as a pastor by trying to convince people of your politics, especially people who are not even from your country. I say this not just to American pastors. I have had non-American pastors passionately lecture me on their thoughts on US politics, views that would alienate half of America, and I hope that is not how they talk with members of their congregation, because they will undermine their own influence as a pastor. So no matter where you are from, leave the politics back home and deal with the only

24

Kingdom that really matters.

I will say that being informed about the situations in the countries represented in your congregation is a good thing. When you can ask a Nigerian how they feel about the elections that just took place, or ask a Filipino if anyone they knew was affected by the recent typhoon, they feel good to know that you are paying attention to their country. I have the privilege of traveling abroad quite frequently and am often able to speak personally about what I most enjoyed in someone's home country or even their home city. If you have been or go to someone's home country, use that as a way to connect on a deeper level. Never speak of all the things you did not like, unless you know the person very well, and they are clearly interested in your honest feedback, and even then, be gracious. Your job as pastor is to love, equip, and disciple these people, and tearing down their home is usually not a good method to employ.

DIFFERENCES IN EXPECTATIONS

Because international churches are comprised of people from many different walks of life, defining the job of an international pastor can be quite difficult.

Members from some parts of the world expect home visits, others expect you to operate as a vicar showing up at community activities and generally being available as needed, while others expect an executive who makes sure the church keeps running, while others may have something else in mind. Because of this, it is important that you and your leadership define your job description and that that is communicated to the church. While you should strive to be "all things to all men", you have your limits, and trying to meet everyone's expectations for what a pastor should be like will likely be impossible.

Some of these differences in expectation will be due to where people are from but some of it may be due to their church background. Overall, a Roman Catholic has a different expectation for a pastor than someone who has been in an emerging church. Some will expect the church and the pastor to have a large role in the convention, if they have come from church's that were part of an association of churches, like most Baptist churches are. While other members may not feel the pastor should spend time away from the church because the staff of the convention should handle convention matters. Much of this comes down to explaining the pastor's role upfront with newcomers and showing sensitivity to the needs of everyone in the church. That said, many people will express their preferences for how the pastor and the church should operate not out of a need but simply out of a desire to be comfortable and maintain what they have grown used to in past churches. These people deserve gentleness, but they also may have to learn to thrive in a new church situation.

OTHER CHALLENGES

Counseling can be difficult when dealing with people from all over the world. You may need to counsel people who are dealing with issues you have never personally dealt with. You may have a person come to you because they are struggling to manage their home without servants, which they had in their last posting, and they feel like their life is falling apart, while someone else comes to you because they are struggling to cope with being thousands of miles from their spouse who is not allowed to join them for at least three years. These are both legitimate struggles to bring to one's pastor, but present unique challenges to the pastor.

Fortunately for me, as a third culture kid, I was able to fit right in here at North Sea. I understand what it is like for children to lose friends every year, for the adults to not be able to get their favorite foods, and for families to be far away from loved ones. But these were still challenges I had to cope with. One of the hardest challenges that I could not truly be prepared for was being there for my children as they are broken hearted when a best friend leaves or wishing they could see their grandparents more often. It is my children's pain that has caused me at times to question if I have made the right choice ministering internationally more than any other factor.

But the longer you live in a place, the more you adapt to the country you live in. You begin to like certain things better in your new country while you learn to put up with other things that used to really get under your skin. As that happens, it can get tiresome to listen to new expats year after year complaining about how rude the locals are, how bad the food is, etc.

Depending on your role in an international church, you will find the adjustment in ministry goes beyond preaching style and small group discussion. A youth event that worked in the US was not sure to draw youth in in the international setting. A men's hunting trip might be great in one setting but not in another. Street preaching might be great in one location and the wrong choice in another. Learning to be sensitive to the uniqueness of your setting is vital to having a healthy ministry. One way to do this is to truly listen to those who have been there longer than you have, and while you may be wary of people who say, "We have always done it this way", when you come to a new country, it is a good idea to listen to them, at least for the first year or two until you are sure you know what you are doing.

Travel is a continual challenge for many international churches. Since the majority of my congregation is employed in the oil industry, they are constantly gone, whether off shore, at offices abroad, or on vacations putting the extra money they make living internationally to good use. This is a wonderful experience for them, but it makes it difficult to run a church when you cannot get regular Sunday school teachers, find a time for your leaders to all meet, or even be relatively sure that the important sermon you want to deliver will be heard by the majority of your church on a normal Sunday.

While this can be very wearing, most of our international churches have to adapt to this to some extent. Easter and Christmas holidays have drastically lower attendance at North Sea. For us, summer is a slow time as many people spend weeks away visiting family in their home countries. We try to take advantage of the breaks as well to rest and recover, plan and get caught up on paperwork, or connect with the families that stay in town on a more personal level through a meal together or an open house on Christmas Eve, since the church is their family here.

Because our people have traveled a lot, many have a concern for other parts of the world. Missions is an area that our church has become very involved in, sending missions teams to different parts of the world as well as funding for numerous projects. This has been a great way to even connect to the home countries of some of our members as a church family. I have tried to embrace what makes the congregation at my church unique instead of complaining, focusing on "sending missionaries on Exxon's payroll", hoping to maximize their effectiveness both at home and abroad.

CHAPTER THREE
TRANSITIONING FROM AN AMERICAN MILITARY CHURCH
TO AN INTERNATIONAL CONGREGATION

Larry J. Jones,
Pastor– 1979-1993
International Baptist Church
Stuttgart, Germany

Larry served the International Baptist Church of Stuttgart, Germany as Senior Pastor for almost 14 years. He earned his Doctor of Ministry in Multi-culturalism from Golden Gate Baptist Theological Seminary. His Master of Divinity is from Southwestern Baptist Theological Seminary and his bachelor's from Howard Payne University. Larry has preached, led seminars and mission trips to 38 countries around the world. He retired after 12 years of service as the Director of Missions for the Lubbock Baptist Association, with 114 member churches, and previously pastored and started churches in Texas. He and his wife Linda are in their retirement years with a focus on their family of 15, which includes 9 grandchildren.

The International Baptist Church of Stuttgart, Germany was initially called the Neckar Valley Baptist Church in Stuttgart, Sindelfingen. It was started in 1961.

Upon my wife's thirty-fourth birthday on November 4, 1979, God called us to serve Neckar Valley. What began as a simple call to serve a small American congregation on foreign soil would lead us upon a complex spiritual journey, which would culminate with a large family of believers comprised of people from over forty different nations around the globe.

This transformation preceded the "Fall of the Wall," the collapse of the Soviet Empire in 1989, and modern globalization. Few international English language churches existed on the planet in the late '70's and early '80s.

The transition from an American military church to an international one, which ensued over the next fourteen years, taught me "the value of one," the value that God places on each individual, regardless of background and status. It was a lesson, which I failed to realize until a penetrating conversation occurred with Ray Reynolds when he powdered me with questions. Until we arrived, Ray was the church's longest serving pastor, and he had only served three years.

"What did God do to cause such a radical transformation?" Ray asked. Our discussion led to the discovery of the "value of one." We pondered, "How did God enable His people to embrace His divine initiative of His own highly held value, the "value of one"?

The Value of One

Neckar Valley was started in 1961 to offer U.S. military personnel and their families an alternative to the chapel experience on local military bases. The church was started for military members by military members. The motive: no interference from governmental governance. They desired to exercise freely what they believed the Bible teaches concerning all matters of doctrine and faith.

Linda and I fell in love with these men and women of faith who lived in Germany as members of the US Armed Forces along beside their families. They loved God. They loved each other.

Our military congregation included one non-military: an American scientist who worked at Max Plank. Don and Leah provided the church a different point of view, especially with the involvement of their four teenagers, none of whom had any military frame of reference.

By the time of our departure we had witnessed how God worked through a small number of Americans to become a large congregation comprised of hundreds of people who represented 40+ nationalities on any given Sunday. Indeed, if I could provide one principle, which was greater than any other, to document how God worked to make this remarkable transformation, I would call it "God's value of one."

God places a high value upon every human being. Through His providential will He is ready to assume full responsibility for anyone who yields his life to Him.

Jesus practiced His Father's "value of one." The Father sent His One and only Son to redeem each and everyone one of us. By sending His Son the Father demonstrated how much He valued me, not to mention you. In like manner the Son on earth valued individuals supremely. The Jesus encounters of the New Testament reveal that when a person discovers his true value in Christ, that person turns to others of like kind and brings them to Jesus. When that same person discovers how God values every individual supremely, he then begins to grasp "God's value of one."

At Jacob's well the Samaritan woman, who had been abused by multiple lust-filled characters, met the Savior, who freed her from her sin-filled life. She brought her entire village to come and see the Man. While this Man knew everything about her horrible past, He accepted her willingly.

Zacchaeus, whose demented personality had demeaned him as much as his diminutive form had damaged his ego, met Jesus. The God-

Man accepted the little man. In turn, Zack immediately called upon his fellow outcasts to have dinner in his home with Jesus. They came.

Yes! Jesus preached to the masses. His heart, however, always bled for the lost sheep, the one who did not make it home with the ninety-nine. The quest of Jesus was and is for the lost sheep, the lost coin and the lost son.

He sought for the woman who "touched" Him, the man born blind, the paralytic, the tax collector, the one demon-possessed, the leper, the Pharisee who came secretly at night, the fisherman, the centurion and on and on the list goes. Because Jesus valued the individual, the individual brought others to Jesus.

Swiss theologian, Karl Barth, called the High and Holy God "Other." Indeed there is no one like God. There is none like Jesus. He alone is "Other." The incredible Truth is that the "Other" seeks "others" who are unlike the "Other." The "others" are unholy and wretched and lost.

The "value of one" is the way Jesus values each and every "other." He is ready to accept anyone who turns to Him in faith.

When we, who are followers of Jesus, value the "other" one, who is not like us, we are practicing a Jesus-principle. The "others," who are not like us must be sought intentionally. They must be sought like Indiana Jones seeks a lost treasure, like the Great Shepherd seeks a lost sheep.

Intentionally we seek the "other" whose culture is different. His language is perhaps different. His taste for food, music, and personal activities are also be different. His clothes maybe different. The color of his skin different as well. He is "other."

When I value highly the "other" who is so different; and then receive him as Jesus does, something radical happens. When this process becomes the normal process of a corporate body of believers, the

32

church becomes an international church.

A Committed Long-term Pastor

During the first eighteen years of the Stuttgart church's life, the church had been led by a plethora of pastors. The longest tenure of any pastor, Ray Reynolds, had been just three years. Indeed it was a transient congregation with transient members as well as transient pastors.

Our pastoral-contract with the church called for a 3-year term, which could be renewed. However, I discovered that no matter how much I discussed the future of the church, no one really believed the church had much of a future. When I spoke of coming out from under the arm of the local German church, which leased their property to us, the church gave it little thought. When I spoke of purchasing our own property, it was always "too far into the future" and an "impossible task." When I spoke of extending our contract beyond three years, it seemed to have little effect. They didn't believe it. It had never happened before. We were all transients.

Prior to our first stateside furlough the deacons and I made an agreement concerning several matters. The two most important matters to me dealt with the location of the pastor's quarters and the name of the church. Their decision was: "After you return we'll discuss these things seriously." It was a "wait-and-see" attitude.

The truth was that they themselves had plans to complete their present assignment and were already thinking of their next military assignment, most likely in another city, if not another continent. Since its inception in 1961 this perpetual rotation of members and leadership was the church's culture. The same was expected of the pastor.

When we returned to Stuttgart from furlough in 1984, the church's culture of the concept of time changed. A sense of permanency came into being. The concept of a "permanent" pastor helped to change the culture of the church. Upon our return we had their permission to begin searching for a new location for the parsonage. This special permission seemed to grant the pastor a new position of authority. It was an earned authority.

New life was given to the church. Although we had always felt a strong love from the church for us, it seemed that their love had deepened. So had ours for them. A new commitment to Christ seemed deeper for us all.

In years to come I would identify this singular event: i.e. our return from furlough and the move of the parsonage to a central location as the most significant pivotal point in the church's history. Today people mistakenly think that the church's miraculous purchase of expensive land and the construction of the facilities as the most significant event. No! The turning point for the church was when a long-term commitment was adopted between pastor and people.

The value of this one church was greatly enhanced. In the providential will of God this church suddenly had great value. Today I recognize that this long-term commitment, which was made in 1984, laid the foundation for a plethora of changes to come.

Including Everyone

Soon after our initial arrival in Stuttgart I discovered that the military personnel in our church were almost exclusively officers. These officers were accustomed to making decisions. They were colonels and majors. It was only natural that they led the church. Indeed, the church was led efficiently, but not necessary effectively.

It startled me that the church had a marked absence of enlisted military personnel. Indeed, it was an interesting observation to note. When an enlisted member visited the church, he may have been warmly received, but he didn't feel accepted. Neither did his young wife.

You see, in the military culture it is highly discouraged for officers to fraternize with enlisted personnel. In the church this subject was never discussed. However, it was revealed to me through my visits in the homes of the enlisted. They felt they were considered inferior to the officers. Hearing the "value of one" preached and practicing the "value of one" are two separate matters. A friendly but brief welcome is distinctly different from a genuine expression of love and acceptance.

I thank God for our Deacon Chairman, Dave, and his wife, Jimmie, who came to realize the church's predicament. They were the first to break the ice. They took the necessary steps to create change. They invited enlisted personnel and their families into their home in their officer's quarters for dinner. They did this frequently.

It didn't take long for the corporate body to follow in this baby step. It was one small step for the church, but one giant leap toward the future. Eventually the church had a broad base of military personnel, including both enlisted and officers. It began with the recognition that all have value in the Kingdom of God. Each and every one has value.

In retrospect I discovered that the "superior" or "dominant" culture must "decrease" so that the "inferior" or "minority" culture might "increase." I call this the "John the Baptist principle." Speaking of the "Other," John said "I must decrease so that He may increase." This spirit of humility leads to the exercise of the "value of the one," who is "other."

This subject brings to mind our only non-military family in the church. Remember? In 1979 there was only one non-military family in the church. Don and Leah, along with their four teenage children, stood out like a sore thumb. Indeed, they were "other."

Unlike military personnel other Americans did not live in compounds. They did not wear uniforms. They did not drive vehicles with identifiable license plates. They did not buy groceries at the commissary. They did not shop at the PX. They did not take European vacations to far away military recreational facilities. Don was the only man in the church whose hair was long. The list seems

35

endless.

This one non-military family inspired us to search for "others." It was like hunting for needles in a haystack. We found them in tiny pockets in society. At first they trickled into the church.

The culture of other Americans who live oversees is distinctly different from the military culture. In the early years the dominant culture of the church had to make some changes in order to allow others to become leaders. Once the cultural shift of "those in charge" shifted, these "other" Americans found their way to the church in good numbers. The church was becoming multi-cultural without fully realizing it. Non-military "Others" were feeling accepted.

Mono-cultural churches become multi-cultural churches one culture at a time. Cultural shifts occur when "the value of one" is practiced authentically.

A New Name: "International"

A young Hungarian family visited our church. Otto and Ari proudly identified themselves as Donau-Schwabs. Donau-Schwabs are actually Germans who descended from the Black Forest, but migrated along the Danube River from western Germany to eastern Transylvania in the Ukraine.

This particular couple was born in communist Hungary. In spite of living in a communist society, which was filled with atheists, they practiced their faith openly in a Baptist church. They sought a way to escape from an oppressive government. (Remember, the Wall had not yet come down.) Though difficult, as a newly married couple they found a way to relocate to the West. In Stuttgart they joined a local German Baptist church. Then came the children.

After years of faithful attendance and in spite of their active involvement in the local German Baptist church, they were never asked to serve in a leadership role. Their Hungarian accents betrayed them. Like the American enlisted men, they felt they were not accepted. These experiences caused them to feel like "foreigners" even though they were actually Germans.

Then they discovered the "American" congregation at Neckar Valley. For several months they visited the church. They expressed to me their fear that their experiences in the "German" church would be repeated in the "American" church. They feared that they would not really be accepted.

We had them in our home for an evening dinner. We talked for hours. When they reciprocated with an evening in their home, they pled with us most humbly, "Would it be acceptable for us to join your American church?"

I wept.

I found it humiliating to realize that such dear people would feel that they had to beg for acceptance into our "American" fellowship. Indeed I felt that our church was filled with loving people, who welcomed others genuinely. I discovered, however, that even the friendliest congregation must overcome perceptions. Perception is everything.

Outsiders feel like outsiders. Foreigners feel like foreigners. Minorities feel like minorities. This is an inescapable fact. This perception must be overcome. *The dominant culture must always take the first step of humility. The dominant culture must lead with authentic humility.* Otherwise, the dominants will always dominate.

When one in the dominant culture values highly the one in the minority culture, he takes great steps to help the "other" overcome perceived feelings. These feelings, which are naturally found in "others" (foreigners, subordinates, refugees, minorities), run deep. Those in the dominant culture must decrease, so that "others" might increase.

The one in the dominant culture must humble himself like Jesus. Jesus left His home in Glory to come to earth. He left his position as a

7-star General to become a lowly "buck-private" (Philippians 2). This attitude is an absolute necessity to practice the "value of one."

The German-Hungarian-Donau-Schwabs joined Neckar Valley. Others like them followed. Soon they were teaching an adult Bible study class for Hungarians. This marked the beginning of an international church.

The "value of one" was widened to include refugees from various countries in North Africa. Members of the church picked them up each Sunday at a refugee center. Church members invited them into their homes for fellowship, food and cultural exchanges. It was radical. It was genuine.

After our return from our first furlough, the church followed my lead to change our name to The International Baptist Church of Stuttgart. At this point, it seemed that the front door of the church burst open widely. With absolutely no advertisement of any kind, the people started coming from everywhere.

Making Adjustments in Programming

The "value of one" soon became common practice. The church became a church for everyone from every nation. While English remained the language of choice during worship, small groups of shared languages met throughout the sanctuary.

Soon a special sound system was purchased. It provided individuals a choice. A person could listen to his own native language in earphones through which an interpreter from English provided. There was never a lack for interpreters.

To celebrate God's love for all nations the church decided to establish a new tradition. Every time a new nation became represented in the church we celebrated with the purchase of a flag from his (her) (their) country. He (she) (they) led the church in worship through a word of testimony or song. The flags were displayed prominently in the church. Once each quarter we celebrated our diversity with a parade of flags. Each native carried his (her) flag proudly during the processional into worship.

Our style of worship began to change regularly. A vast variety of music and musical instruments were utilized. Those who were baptized were asked how they would like to be baptized and by whom. Their native culture was respected and displayed in the manner in which they were baptized.

Believers from various countries were asked to plan the observance of the Lord's Supper. I had never realized that there were so many ways to do this. Often the worship leaders wore their native costumes and requested that their friends do the same. We learned how to worship God more authentically by following the leadership of our newcomers.

Individuals from more than 40 nations came to be represented in the church on any given Sunday. It was phenomenal. A new public address system was purchased to facilitate multiple simultaneous translations through the use of headphones and individual interpreters, who sat in the rear of the church to speak through the system. The weekly worship experience itself was a celebration of God's love.

This is my story of "the value of one."

I, too, consider myself to be a valued one, not because of who I am, but because of Whose I am. When Jesus came to earth I became highly valued. When God chose me to be His, I became more valued. When God called me to be His servant, I became His valued one "for such a time as this" (Esther 4:14).

God's "value of one" is what we must consider in everyone. Each individual is extraordinarily valuable to God. Therefore we who are His must consider each one in humanity of great value. We must humble ourselves by decreasing our own importance in order to increase the importance of the "other."

CHAPTER FOUR
RESPONDING TO THE CALL TO SERVE AN
INTERNATIONAL CHURCH OVERSEAS

By Harry Lucenay
Pastor, Kowloon International Baptist Church
Kowloon Tong, Hong Kong

Harry Lucenay has served as senior pastor of Kowloon International Baptist Church in Hong Kong since 2003. Prior to that he served as pastor at First Baptist Church, Longview, Texas; First Baptist San Antonio, Texas; and Temple Baptist Church, Hattiesburg, Mississippi. He is a graduate of Baylor University, Southwestern Baptist Theological Seminary, and New Orleans Baptist Theological Seminary. He and his wife, Nancy have three grown children, Jonathan, Elise and Charles, and ten grandchildren. The Lucenays are active in the Baptist World Alliance and in mission work in SE Asia.

I looked over the balcony rail of the NTT International House at Hong Kong Baptist University. The buildings along Victoria Harbor stood at a distance with the green mountains behind them. Two thoughts clashed in my mind. First, "What will it be like working here if I do not have a return ticket in my pocket?" Second, "Where does a Texan find space in a place like this?"

August 2002 the pastor search committee from Kowloon International Baptist Church, Kowloon Tong, Hong Kong contacted me about serving as their pastor. I knew nothing about the church. I did not know they had my name. After initial talks, my wife and I visited the city and the church. My own heart was filled with mixed emotions. Two of my children were in university. One was married. Hong Kong is a long way from Texas.

No sense of direction came to me until after I told the church "no" in response to their invitation to come. Then, God became very clear in his communication with me. We accepted the call with confidence. We arrived in Hong Kong the day the health authorities discovered the index patient for SARS. We had no idea the scope of the panic we were soon to encounter.

Kowloon International Baptist Church is located in Kowloon Tong on the peninsula across from Hong Kong Island. Our area of the city was once the home of many British residents. Our church is located between two separated sections of Hong Kong Baptist University. We are a block from the Hong Kong Baptist Hospital. Across the street is an old British army camp that today houses a token presence of People's Republic of China soldiers.

Our fifty-year-old church facilities are quite small. The entire office space we work from would fit in many of the Sunday School classrooms of churches I served in the US. In fact, my office is the size of the private toilet area in the pastor's office of my former pastorate. The building is only partially air conditioned, has limited heat in the coldest part of the year, and enjoys parking for six cars on weekdays with none available on Sundays. That said we do enjoy the privilege of having our own building.

The church staff I inherited included a bi-lingual secretary who was the unofficial assistant pastor of the church, a couple of caretakers and a Minister of Education with no training or experience in his position.

The church family greeting me when I became the pastor of the church wore masks for the first few months after my arrival. The Asian culture is very concerned about spreading germs on others. One of our first decisions was to install sinks outside so people could wash their hands when entering and leaving the church. When people felt the danger of SARS was over, they took off their masks and expected me to know their names. Since most had black hair and dark eyes, putting names to masked faces was a bit of a challenge.

What should a person consider when exploring oversees work?

Expect differences. All overseas churches are not the same any more than all American churches are the same. Some international churches are made up primarily of ex-patriots who are looking for a faith community on foreign soil. Many international churches have varying degrees of mixed cultures within the congregation. Congregations react to cultural differences and class structures differently.

Every church in America has her own culture. The same is true around the world. My venture into Hong Kong carried me into an Asian international church in which I became the first non-missionary pastor. Previously, all pastors had been missionaries under the Foreign Mission Board or the International Mission Board of the Southern Baptist Convention. Before I came to the church, official affiliation with the Southern Baptist Convention entities was discontinued through a peaceful decision. The church was clearly connected with the Hong Kong Baptist Convention. Most of the members had no real idea what any convention relationship meant.

Be aware of your support needs. Going overseas to serve without a mission support entity did raise issues for me. No longer would my annuity be handled by the Annuity Board (GuideStone). Where would my health care come from? If I died, would any American support group reach out to my wife Nancy? If I moved overseas, would I have enough money in my retirement account when I retired?

We spent thirty-five years serving in US pastorates. The people who nurtured us as children in the churches of our childhood needed care as seniors. Most of the younger people in those great churches did not know us. We did not feel right in pushing ourselves on previous churches where we served. Thus, as far as a home base went, we had no stateside church to call home.

When I served Temple Baptist Church, Hattiesburg, MS our missionaries, Ralph and Cora Joyce Davis would come home. They spoke to the church as expected. They met with other missionaries serving elsewhere in the world. Temple, their home church, explored ways to assist their ministry. If one is not a missionary, none of that support is available when serving overseas. The support groups see you as a pastor even as people speak of you as a missionary.

Few Christian conferences are held in great cities like ours. Leadership training and ministerial retreats with other ministers are not common. We have had a few meetings of English pastors serving in Asia but travel cost is a prevailing issue. The European pastors are said to have a stronger network. Several mission boards have offered to allow us to attend their mission meetings at our expense. However, these meetings are designed for their personnel as they should be. The Cooperative Baptist Fellowship has created ways to help us address the retirement fund issue. At the time we came, Jack Snell of CBF promised CBF care for my wife if something happened to me. That was encouraging. He has since retired and gone to be with our Lord. We do not have any ties with the people in CBF mission offices today. But we do have ties with their Church Benefit Board. We have also developed a good relationship with the Baptist World Alliance. This is not a sending organization, but it has given us the opportunity to work with native people in different lands. Insights from dialogue with them have been extremely valuable in our personal development.

I created a small newsletter that I send out most weeks. This helps me document some of the actions of God in our lives and the activities of our city and country as well as to present some prayer needs. I send it to friends and acquaintances who have asked to receive it. Their affirmation, prayer support and encouragement are a great blessing returning to me.

Live in Constant Change: Change touches every part of our ministry. I left ministries in which I had one or two personal secretaries to type and handle much of my administrative work. In the new setting, my secretary's skills were people skills. With the bulletin to type and the data entries of the normal week plus the various governmental issues she needed to handle, she had her hands full.

Over the years we have worked with several secretaries and ministry assistants. They have not been native English speakers. Language difficulties are significant. But the issue goes much deeper. The international church does not always do things as individual Chinese churches do them. And I have not been trained as the local Chinese pastors have been trained. The result introduces a variety of forms of miscommunication between this international pastor and people who have grown up in the local Chinese churches. What is said is not what is heard and what is heard is not what is understood. What is understood is often unrelated to what is meant. What is expected differs in the mind of the speaker and the hearer. Confusion reigns.

The lack of infrastructure is an issue I face repeatedly. Today's staff must serve in the assigned ministry role and handle most of their own secretarial work. In the large church, smaller issues never reach the pastor. In the international church, few of them miss the pastor.

Change entered the pulpit as well. When I discovered most of my congregation spoke English as a second language, I explored and began to preach with PowerPoint. Prior to coming to Hong Kong, I had only preached with PowerPoint once. Now, every Sunday morning the message is accompanied by a slide presentation and sermon notes. (This would not be possible if the church had not agreed to allow me to use my mornings for study.) And I am fortunate to have a wife who enjoys creating the slide presentations. I type my own sermon notes. We believe communication is worth the effort. We do know the messages are carried into many parts of the world each week as our people travel as well as through the Internet.

KIBC has had to make some worship changes as well. We buried the 8:30AM traditional service so we could give birth to a well-received 9:30AM praise and worship service. The 11:00AM service remained traditional. The immediate result of that change brought a significant increase in the attendance in the early service and more people immediately filled any vacated places in the late service.

Committees opened my eyes to more changes. Early in my ministry in Hong Kong, one committee was unanimously in support of a recommendation. About fifteen minutes after the meeting, one member came to me expressing "concern" over the decision. Soon, another called to express the same. By noon the next day, I discovered the committee was unanimous but not in the way I thought. I was beginning to learn some of the ways of my new culture. No one wanted to offend anyone else. Everyone wanted the other to save face. And all wanted to please the pastor. The direct approach of the western church does not always appear in Asian committees. Our people work hard to respect one another and give face to each other. They are usually very considerate of people who might see things differently. This does not mean they give license to wrongdoing. It does mean they try to understand why people say and do what they say and do. Not all international churches share this characteristic.

Like many churches, KIBC had a few people forming key leadership and making most of the decisions. Though they said they wanted to change that, they did not seem to know a healthy process. Anyway, if the pastor were the leader, what difference would it make? We took two to three years discussing possibilities of changing deacon election and committees. When we finally made some small but significant changes, the people were pleased with the process and with the result.

One of the changes that does not meet the eye should be mentioned. When I entered the ministry, serving as pastor of "First Church Big" was an unspoken dream of many young pastors. I have been fortunate enough to serve some rather large churches, large in facilities, large in numbers, large in resources and large in influence. When serving "First Church Big," people turn to speak to you. It can give an inflated sense of importance. Moving around the world to serve in a very small building requires heart work.

One day I was talking with Joshua, a Korean Christian. In referring to KIBC, I said, "It doesn't look much like a church." He asked, "What does a church look like?" When I welcome people as they visit church for the first time in their lives, I know what the ministry should feel like. When I look at the faces of the people hungry to hear God's Word, I know what a church looks like. When I hear their faith discovery stories, I know what the church sounds like. When I see them give sacrificially to help those who have lost everything, I know what church acts like. When I hear them pray for their lost family members and friends, I know what a church sounds like. These sights and sounds stir the soul with warmth that bricks and mortar can never touch.

We had to change some of our family traditions. We stay in Hong Kong for Christmas Eve and Christmas Day services. The church allows me to take 12 days after Christmas for family time, which is not vacation time. They cover my plane fare back to the US for one trip each year. (For many years, they did this for one trip every other year.) We pay for the trips at other times. We now enjoy family Christmas the week after Christmas. (Please note that the Chinese culture makes much more out of Chinese New Year than Americans make out of the calendar New Year. This would not be true of all cultures meaning the difference in traditions would affect what a family might or might not do.)

Since coming to Hong Kong, my father has died and Nancy's mother has died. For several years, I was able to talk with my octogenarian mother almost daily. I was thankful to have siblings living near her.

She died this past year and our church was very gracious to allow me to spend some time with her near the end of her journey on earth. When Dad died, I raced home for the funeral and returned to Hong Kong almost immediately after the services. In so doing, I did not give myself time to process what had happened in my life with his passing. When mom died, I made a special effort to spend more time addressing this major life event. My wife was also able to spend quite a bit of time with her mom the last year of her life.

Our eldest son and his wife have experienced two miscarriages during the time we've been in Hong Kong. The distance from family during crisis times was and is hard. We do talk each week and we use SKYPE liberally so we can see the grandchildren as we talk with them. When I begin to think of the changes in our family, we have seen many from a distance. Shortly after we arrived in Hong Kong, our youngest son became the bear trainer at Baylor University. He was responsible for the feeding and care of two 350-pound bears. His two years in that role greatly affected our prayer life.

Since we have been in Hong Kong, our other two children have married. The three couples have produced ten children. Nancy has been able to be present for a few of the births. I was only able to be present for the birth of the tenth, which happened to be in Texas where my mother was spending her last days. The arrival of grandchildren has certainly had a pull on our hearts. (And the presence of grandchildren greatly affects the way potential staff considers moving to Hong Kong.)

Personal Growth: Discover ways to stretch with God. When I was considering coming to Hong Kong a friend said he had to discover that "everyone has to be somewhere. I am here and that is okay." Those words have come back to my mind many times. Frankly, I am glad I am where God has placed me. When I came, I decided God had more to teach me than I had to teach others. This meant I needed to be a learner. One of the first things a good learner must learn to say is "yes." I decided to say "yes" as often as I could. Many times people come to me and the voices of experience would shout "no" through the tight muscles in my gut. But I would go through my checklist. "Is anything wrong with this biblically?" "Is it going to hurt anyone?" "What is the problem in letting this happen?" If the answers to those questions could be defended, I let people go. No catastrophes. In fact, God has stretched our people while he has stretched me.

I do not mean to say, I have discarded my training and experience. I am seeking to explore ways what I know can be stretched, improved and reworked with the freshness of God's grace.

Our people continue to teach me about their culture. The lessons I am learning teach me more about both the people I serve and the God who loves all of us. Sure, I miss my family. I miss driving on the right side of the road. I miss the Star Spangled Banner playing before a football game. I miss Saturday afternoon American football and March Madness. I miss Tex-Mex and bluebonnets. But for all those cultural things I miss, I am making new discoveries that are helping me grow at a stage in life when the temptation would lead one to go on "cruise control."

God uses differences to expand our understanding. Some parts of America are like a monoculture. Others are like a patchwork quilt. Hong Kong is a hotpot of blending cultures. Differences do not label one better than any other. Learning to work with diversity creates the setting in which God's symphony of humanity can audition.

Establish your new base. Before we moved to Hong Kong, the church allowed us to make some suggestions on the renovations of the 40-year-old flat they provide for the pastor. We made our place very comfortable for Americans with a touch of China. When our children come to visit us they see enough of the home in which they grew up to feel at home. We needed that to help us "escape" the "culture shock" and feel at home. Guests to our home find both American and Chinese influence, which communicates acceptance and appreciation to those who are Chinese.

Hong Kong remains quite friendly to Westerners. Not every city in the world speaks English. Not every city is a shoppers' paradise, an electronics center or a tourist destination. Not every city has easy access. We realize we could have easily faced more difficulties in other locations.

Making ourselves at home means developing friendships. We have Western friends and Asian friends. In fact, we have friends from many parts of the world. These friendships share each day's realities with us. In sharing, the people who accompany us use their experiences and cultural backgrounds to inform our interpretation of what is taking place in the world near and far.

Explore the culture of your new assignment. People everywhere like to know you know about them. When I moved from Texas to Mississippi, the people were pleased when I read a Mississippi history textbook. Chinese people welcome our exploration of their history, home country, food and cultural events. We work hard to recognize and follow the proper patterns of behavior as well as the spoken and unspoken rules. People everywhere appreciate the efforts newcomers make to learn their language. Our international congregation loves it when we visit the various countries they call home.

Expect to read the Bible with "new eyes." Our study of culture has awakened us to the emphasis on "shame and honor." All my education took place in the southern United States. My exposure to Christianity and the Bible occurred in the "Bible-belt." As a result, my views and vocabulary have been strongly influenced by concepts of "guilt and righteousness." Not until I stepped into the community structure where "shame and honor" prevail did I begin to see the scriptural references to shame in a different light. Confucius uses rules and ritual practices to push people toward excellence. If they failed, they hurt the community. People maintain respectability by doing what is expected of them.

The shame I was acquainted with was more a reaction to criticism and a failure to live up to obligations. Sometimes the shame was the result of getting caught. The Bible addresses both guilt and shame as well as fear. In my attempts to connect with the people whose approach to life was developed in a collective environment with a strong sense of shame and honor, I found a need for more exposure to the biblical message on shame.

The exploration of shame not only entered my evangelism at the point of theology but it also related to the way people considered the gospel. My individualistic approach to guilt and righteousness missed the inner struggle of my people as they considered the claims of Jesus. For some were reared to offer food to their ancestors every day and especially on some ritualistic days. If these people submitted to Jesus, they would bring shame to their parents by rejecting family tradition. Others saw the failure to worship the family idols as a form of shame.

Learn to listen to what you are saying with different ears. Illustrations and idioms may not communicate in a different culture. For three years I had translators who were students in Hong Kong Baptist University. They were studying translation and helped with the English to Mandarin translation of the early service. Every Thursday I met with the translator to walk through the sermon notes. Some of these translators had no Christian background. I spent extra time with them explaining what words and Bible stories meant. When we encountered an idiom I often asked them for something similar in Chinese. They frequently had excellent suggestions. Sometimes when I related a story, they told me a similar Chinese story. Their insights helped me connect with my congregation. We had an excellent linguist listen to their translations on the headphones. She would help them with anything they failed to translate properly.

Avoid debt. If you cannot afford to do something or to buy whatever you think you need, do not use your credit to go into bondage. One of our basic commitments to a healthy lifestyle was to avoid anything that would put us on the "monthly payment" merry-go-round. Living overseas we could easily see ways what we had in other ministries or "back home" could make our ministry so much better. However, the freedom from debt has helped us live more generously than we would have otherwise lived. And this freedom has removed the worries over how to escape the weight of yesterday's financial decisions.

Pay attention to your health. Our move to Hong Kong brought us into a culture that loves to eat. Our parents had taught us to eat everything on our plates. In a Chinese culture, if you eat everything on your plate, people will keep putting things on your plate. We had to learn to leave things on our plates. We had to learn the first dish or dishes on the table were not the last dishes we would see.

We had to work to find time to exercise. Physical exercise is critical to a healthy ministry. Failure to find some way to exercise will feed burnout and a variety of physical problems. I'm no athlete, but paying attention to what I eat and getting a little exercise does make a significant difference. Living in this part of the world does involve more walking than we did in the normal daily experiences in the US. However, I would do well to improve in both of these areas.

I also have seen the need for rest. A growing church always has something else that needs to be done. Sometimes you have to step away from the endless "to do" lists and refocus. Reading, rest and some relaxation can restore your physical and mental health. They also serve as good reminders that "all" the ministry does not depend on you. If it does, something is wrong in the way you are doing ministry.

Hong Kong has many forms of entertainment, good and unacceptable, expensive and reasonable. Nancy and I have found we had to recreate our date times to make us leave the computers and set aside the work, so we could spend time with each other. We also make a big issue of not messing with our phones and turning off the television when we eat together. The answering machine will pick up any calls you need to return. You can do that in a timely fashion and still give your attention to your mate. (If you were counseling someone, you would not answer the phone. Why should you rob your mate and family of the few minutes you have together around the table?)

Remember your taxes. If you enter a country like Hong Kong, you may discover you will have taxes in the country where you are living as well as taxes in the United States. KIBC made arrangements to address my Hong Kong taxes so that I would only have to be responsible for the US taxes. I am older and do not have young children in school. If I had children going to a private, English-speaking school in Hong Kong, their tuition would be considered part of my salary when figuring taxes. This would have been a financial nightmare.

Consider your health care insurance. We have very good health care in Hong Kong. Not every country does. We were able to get a Hong Kong-based healthcare provider. However, we have employed some retired Ministers of Education. They could not get a locally provided healthcare policy. To consider going back to the US for healthcare needs would be out of the question. We have been able to arrange healthcare travel policies that have worked well for these employees. Since they usually return to the US at least once a year (sometimes at their own expense), they are able to comply with the travel policy requirements.

Collect good resources for your ministry. I think we have about 1000 books in our flat. We definitely have several hundred more on the "Kindle" app on our iPads. We have a good library of books on China. I am partial to https://www.logos.com/ for my study library. I like the system of cross references they provide and the ease with which I can find what I am searching for in my resources. Some like WordSearch. And others use a variety of free offerings on the Internet. When I came to Hong Kong, I went to the Hong Kong Baptist Seminary Library to see what was available there. I knew I needed to read to improve in the ministry God has given me.

I made an agreement with our congregation that allows me to study in the mornings unless there is an emergency or funeral. This has been a blessing to the pastor and the people. My people know they will get "new sermons" every week. In fact, they have the sermon notes for almost twelve years of sermons and they will tell you the sermons they get are not reruns. Even when an old text is used, the sermon is new.

Pastors do well to keep reading. Education is a life-long process. The things that worked in ministry when I first began do not work the same way. The things that worked in country churches do not always fit city churches. Every church is different. Every ministry is different. And every season in a minister's life is different. Keep your mind fresh and everyone will benefit.

Do not expect outside income from your ministry overseas. In the US, the minister may be paid for performing weddings or funerals or for leading in revivals. Overseas, the culture may not consider any obligation in this regard. On the few occasions I have been asked about my "fees," I have told the person, "The church pays my salary and you need not worry about me." They have been shocked due to the many other expenses they are facing at these critical moments. Invitations to speak may or may not provide an honorarium. And churches employing you may or may not expect you to return any honorarium to them since you are employed by them "full-time."

You may discover that your church does not recognize special occasions the way these occasions were recognized in the US. There may be no Christmas gift or anniversary recognition. If there is such, it may take the form of a meal or a plaque or something else symbolic of the culture. Set your heart to enjoy their appreciation in their language.

Learn their language. We took language lessons the first year in Hong Kong. We yielded to time demands and ended our weekly lessons at that time. One of our regrets is not learning the local language. Yes, we live in an English friendly city. But learning the language is one of the ways of communicating acceptance to people.

Keep your church involved in missions. One of the best ways to keep your people involved in missions is to lead them. Take mission teams to different countries in your area. The constant exposure of our church to mission projects helps our people see themselves as people who are involved in God's work, not just the receivers of what others can do in God's work. We had to teach the church that we could do our own Vacation Bible School. The church captured that concept and never looked back. The pastors before me took teams to various mission fields. I have done the same. The people return excited and spiritually refreshed. And they give to missions. Our people had given to missions according to the monthly designations set up by Southern Baptists in the United States. Home Missions was a March offering and Foreign Missions was a December offering. We had to work to combine both offerings for a November/December giving time. And it took a real step of faith to set the offering goal by looking at the church budget and making our goal 10% of the regular budget. But we have regularly given a mission offering equaling 13-15% of our regular budget offering. Please note this is separate from the church budget.

One of the beautiful experiences we had with mission giving took place in 2008. Typhoon Nargis wreaked havoc in Myanmar in early May that year. The first Sunday in May, we began a collection for relief that we planned to send through the Baptist World Aid team. The next week a huge earthquake tore into Sichuan Province of China. The Hong Kong news played pictures of the devastation day after day. I felt we should become involved in this disaster relief with an unusual offering. We decided to take an offering for Earthquake Relief in addition to the offering for Typhoon Relief. On the Sunday of the offering, all the money received would go to these relief efforts. The only way one could give to KIBC would be through a designated gift. The plan was announced. The people prayed. The people gave an offering equal to about 40% of the church's annual budget. To God be the Glory! And, yes, our budget gifts never missed a beat.

Find good Bible study materials. We are primarily an English language church. Our Sunday School/Bible Study uses English literature, except for our Cantonese department. However, much of the available English literature is written to an American audience.

Sometimes the situations, illustrations and applications do not fit with our culture. This is also true with regard to some of the Vacation Bible School literature.

Growing a strong Sunday School/Bible Study requires good materials and good teachers. Most of the church year we try to coordinate the sermon series with the Sunday School/Bible Study literature. The pastor usually chooses the direction he wants to take in the pulpit and the hunt is on for good literature to support that series. In my sermon preparation, I work very hard to allow the teachers to use the literature helps that go with the studies we provide. I do my study from other sources and seek to bring meaningful insights that do not "steal the thunder" of the teachers. Our people have responded well to this Bible study approach.

I left my last pastorate in the United States after taking an offer of severance. Earlier in my ministry, I had been called to serve a church that had been devastated by a power struggle. The brokenness touched everything the church sought to do. I did not want to be any part of a war between Christians. Rather than wrestle with a power struggle, I stepped aside. A lady stopped me in the middle aisle of the church after I preached my last sermon there. She asked, "Now, what are you going to do." I said, "For thirty-five years I have been challenging people to 'Trust God.' Now, I get to 'Trust God.'" (It's one thing to "Trust God" when you have a job. It's something completely different to "Trust God" when you do not have a job and people wonder what the real reason is behind your departure from your previous church.)

The following year was a year of self-discovery. The journey was not easy. I was surprised at how much of my identity was tied to my work. However, I sought to be open to what God wanted to do with my life. Opportunities to serve the Lord in stateside churches came open. But I could not find God's hand in those invitations. The idea of serving internationally had lingered in my mind. But I thought this might happen as an interim pastor in retirement.

God has used Hong Kong to introduce me to immeasurably more than all I could ask or imagine. After a dozen years of ministry in the 10/40 window I am deeply grateful for this privilege. Without the severance I may or may not have given the proper attention to praying about the opportunity of coming here. With the severance and the strong sense that God wanted me to stay in local church ministry, I cannot imagine a more rewarding ministry.

CHAPTER FIVE
PLANTING CHURCHES IN THE SHADOW OF CATHEDRALS
INTERNATIONAL CHURCH PLANTING IN EUROPE

Rev. Bob Marsh
Pastor/Church Planter,
Converge International Fellowship, Darmstadt, Germany
Church Planting Ministry Coordinator,
International Baptist Convention

Bob Marsh has served in Europe since 2011 as the church planting pastor of Converge International Fellowship in Darmstadt, Germany. Prior to that he served as planter/pastor of Gateway Community Church in Mayville, Wisconsin for 16 years. He was born in West Virginia, raised in Ohio and studied at St. Paul Bible College and Liberty University Seminary. Bob and his wife Carol have three children and three grandchildren, all of whom live in the USA.

On the day of Pentecost, Acts 2:5 tells us that "There were God-fearing Jews from every nation under heaven" in the city of Jerusalem. The presence of such an international population gave the newly-Spirit-filled followers of Jesus an amazing opportunity to fulfill His command to "make disciples of all nations" while the words were still fresh in their ears. What must have seemed like an impossible task just days previously was suddenly made possible by the Sovereign work of God in *bringing the nations to them!*

Twenty centuries later that work of God is being repeated, as people "from every nation under heaven" gather in cities around the globe. Nowhere is that more evident than in Europe. London is consistently listed as the most international city in the world, with more than 160 language groups. It is followed by other European metro areas like Brussels, Paris, Berlin, Amsterdam and Munich. Each of those cities has hundreds of thousands, if not multiple millions of international citizens, most of whom speak English to some degree. Of course this is true around the world, but Europe occupies a key position between Asia and the Americas, is in the same time-zone as much of Africa, and in the post-9/11 world offers easier entry for work or study than the United States.

As a result, even small and mid-sized cities in Europe can present an opportunity to make disciples of every nation through the strategic planting of International, English-language churches. Our call to church planting in Darmstadt, Germany drew plenty of raised eyebrows, confused looks and the question, "Where"? Why that city?" But we have found that even with its relatively small population of 175,000, Darmstadt hosts an international population from more than 140 nations on every continent. Students, scientists and business professionals are drawn by he world-renowned *Technische Universität Darmstadt*, the Operations Center of the European Space Agency, and the *Technische-Zone Rhein-Main*, the largest technology park in Germany.

Of course, planting a church is based on far more than demographics. Jesus pointed out that a wise person will do their research, count the cost and evaluate the obstacles before make a decision – even a decision to follow Him. (Luke 14:28-33) It stands to reason that a follower of Christ should continue to use similar wisdom in serving their Master.

Pray

It has often been said that, "Prayer is not the least we can do; it is the most we can do." That is especially true when venturing into church planting. Jesus promised His disciples in Matthew 16 that He would build His church. Included in that declaration is the assurance that, "the gates of Hades will not overcome it." This implies that those gates will indeed be attempting to destroy the church. Dr. Marvin Vincent points out that the disciples would have understood those words to mean that the "councils of the Satanic powers...confront and assault the church which Christ will build upon the rock."[9]

Spiritual warfare is a greater part of church planting than location, vision casting or fund-raising. The attack of the enemy is relentless and varied. It may be mechanical (cars, home appliances, or computers), economical (job-loss, unexpected tax burden, repairs), physical (unexpected illness, sudden injury or a chronic condition), emotional (depression, anxiety, marital stress), or spiritual (weakened faith, "distance" from God, conflict among spiritual mentors). Whatever tact he may take, we can be certain that the forces of darkness will do all they can to overcome the advancement of the kingdom of light.

Prayer and fasting are the keys to victory. There are some issues of spiritual warfare that can only be won through these two oft-neglected disciplines. (Daniel 9&10, Mark 9:29) Each step of the process of church planting, from first sensing God's call to the launch and establishment of the new church, must be accompanied by seasons of prayer and fasting.

Closely aligned with the personal disciplines listed above is the enlisting of a team of intercessors who will become partners in the ministry by consistently and faithfully keeping the church planter, his family and the church in their prayers. Our initial efforts as church planters included the recruiting at least 100 individuals who

---

[9] Marvin R. Vincent, D.D., *Word Studies in the New Testament* (Grand Rapids, MI: Eerdmans Publishing Co., 1973), 96.

would covenant to keep us in their regular times of prayer. These faithful friends were available to receive emails, letters and even phone calls when the darkness seemed overwhelming! Paul, the father of church planting, knew this dynamic well. He often called on the churches to "strive together with me in your prayers to God on my behalf." (Rom 15:30, 1 Cor ,Phil 1:9, 22)

Picture

One of the things to pray for early in the process is a picture of God's heart for the community to which He has called you. What vision has God placed within your heart? Is it an international student ministry, focused on business professionals and their families, targeted toward refugees and under-served immigrants, or a combination of all of the above? Each of those segments is easily found throughout Europe, and God's heart is drawn toward all of them, and many more – which has he impassioned you to reach? When you close your eyes and consider the call of God on your heart to plant a church – what picture comes to mind? That vision will not only focus your efforts, it will enable you to find partners in the ministry.

Partner

We've already talked about the necessity of prayer partners. They are essential, but many more partners are needed in the effort to plant churches. This is especially true of Europe, which has perhaps the most "passively hostile" environments toward the church. Europe is not only the "most un-evangelized" continent of the world (less than 4%) – it is much worse. Centuries of marginal familiarity with the Christian story have led to deep-seated contempt for the faith and the faithful.

At social events, business professionals and students will initially be engaging and interested in telling about their work, study and lives. When they inquire about your work, and the subject of the church is raised, the demeanor quickly changes. It is not politely dismissive in most cases, but contemptuous. Previously interested expressions turn quickly to disrespect and even condescension. The church is held in very low regard in Europe, partly because of the tax-financed State church and partly because of the abuses of the past.

Europeans face the most difficult of obstacles to overcome: prosperity and self-sufficiency. The financial, social and individual success and affluence of the average European has led him to dismiss the need for and existence of God. "If there is a God," an executive of Deutsche Telekom once told me, "He expects me to solve my own problems, not to bring them to him in prayer and ask him to deal with them!"

In such an atmosphere, the church planter can feel terribly alone...and often they are! Walking the church-lined streets of a city in Europe, in the shadow of magnificent cathedrals, it is difficult to find other believers. Finding those who are concerned with reaching out to their neighbors, co-workers and friends is even more difficult.

Which is all the more reason why making such partnerships is critical! Even as gifted and effective as the Apostle Paul was, he did not plant churches alone. He travelled with Barnabus, Silas, Luke, and Timothy. He quickly partnered with new or existing followers of Jesus in his efforts – often moving newly converted disciples of Christ into the work. Pastor Jim Putman, a former wrestler (often mistakenly thought to be an "individual" sport), wrote a book entitled, "Church is a Team Sport."[10] If that is true, and it is, then church planting is even more dependent upon vital partnerships.

Identifying and connecting with churches and individuals of like conviction was critical in our work of church planting in Germany. By God's grace we found favor with an existing, 100-year-old church that immediately made their facility available to us for weekly worship services. Even more importantly, they became *partners* in our work. They include our service and a link to our website on their home page, they have invited us to partner with them in the bi-annual "Night of Churches" in our community, have invited us to preach from their pulpit and included us in ministries of the church.

---

[10] Jim Putman, Church is a Team Sport (Grand Rapids, MI: Baker Books, 2008).

We have also found pastors and individuals from other local indigenous churches who have welcomed us to their city and their mission to evangelize the region. These are, in some ways, the "people of peace," that Jesus instructed his disciples to identify as He sent them from village to village.

Equally important is connecting with other regional International Churches. The first person we visited with upon our arrival was the pastor of another English-language Baptist church in our city. We assured him that it was not our intention to swap sheep with his flock, but to reach out to those who were disconnected from Christ and His church. We talked about ways we could work together, support one another and exemplify Christ's love. When that church closed, after 40 years of service to the city, and 20 years on the field by the pastor and his family, they recommended and encouraged their people to join us in our fellowship and mission.

Place

Finding a partner church can often open doors for a location for the new church to meet for worship. Before jumping too quickly at the first opportunity that comes along, it is important to prayerfully consider the many dynamics that impact a church location in Europe. The vast majority of international students, many of the business and educational professionals, and most all refugees will be without a car. They are very expensive, fuel is more than twice the cost of the United States, and insurance can be equally oppressive. Those facts provide the church planter with a challenge that must not be ignored – the location of worship services, small groups, social activities, and even their apartment must be easily accessible to the target population.

Thankfully, the realities of European life have had a dramatic impact on the culture. Europe has a wonderful system of public transportation, and a nearly universal reliance on bicycles. When considering the location of a worship site, or an apartment for the church planter and their family, it is critical that each be near a public transportation hub – a bus stop, tram or train station, or at least a bike trail.

Provide

When the church planter has prayed and sought the heart of God for their target city, captured a picture of the mission, identified partners and located a place, it is essential that the work begin to deliver the goods! What type ministry the church provides will depend in large part on the specific target that God has placed in the heart. The ministry provided to business professionals will be vastly different from that offered to refugees, and even to graduate level students.

But there is a common thread that will run through virtually every ministry plan – and is a vital part of international church ministry – the establishment of genuine and sincere relationships. People who find themselves permanently or temporarily located in a foreign environment are terribly lonely. Many of the students we encounter are appreciative of the opportunity they have been given, but they are often times away from their family, friends and culture for the first time. The heavy demand of their studies, and the pressure of immediate dismissal if they fail causes an intensity of commitment to their studies. As a result, social interaction, even in the dormitories and student housing facilities, is rare.

Business professionals are often on temporary assignment at great expense to their company, and the demands and expectations are accordingly high. They work long hours, and often return to a lonely apartment (sometimes not much more than a hotel room), where they are confronted by neighbors, restaurants, television and radio that is in a language they do not speak. As a result, many retreat to the cocoon of their room, open a laptop and spend lonely hours longing for personal contact – and home.

That circumstance is even more acute for the spouse of those professionals who is occasionally given the opportunity to join their partner on a short-term European assignment. As great as such a chance might sound at first glance, the reality is that their working spouse is often overwhelmed by long hours at work, and the spouse, unable to work on their guest visa, finds themselves for weeks alone and "trapped" in their apartment – often with young children who miss their friends and grandparents. This situation puts an understandable strain on the marriage, and has resulted in more than one spouse returning home with the children for the duration of the overseas assignment.

The plight of refugees is even worse. Suffering from the trauma of being forced to flee their home and family, with little or no hope of return, and often no source of gainful employment, the feelings of loneliness and hopelessness are exponentially greater.

The international church in Europe has the opportunity and the responsibility to provide ministry care and compassion to each of these situations – and more! While ministries may take a nearly endless variety of programmatic shapes and styles, the core remains the same: people need to feel valued, noticed and loved. Students need an occasional home-cooked meal and a movie night with friends. Professionals need to be invited for lunch or dinner and to be *listened to.* Their spouses need contact with others in their situation. They need to be taken around the city, shown how the public transportation works, how to buy groceries in a foreign language and culture, and invited to join with other stay at home spouses during the long and lonely days.

Sabotaging this seemingly obvious truth is the feeling that for the church planter and the regular, long-term members of the church family, there is a temptation to insulate one's self from such short-term relationships because of the pain that will inevitably come when relationship comes to a conclusion. The average stay for a student or professional in an international church is three years. That equates to a lot of "goodbyes and farewells." In our preparation to plant in Europe, the single most common answer to the question, "What is the most difficult part of church planting in Europe?" was, "Saying 'goodbye' to everyone as they leave!"

The church planter must be very careful to keep a tender heart. To be willing to face the pain of separation in the face of their call to minister to those in need. And it is important that they model that behavior and attitude for their congregation. It must be taught and reinforced until the realization of this key aspect of ministry is embedded deeply in the DNA of the new church family. Theodore Roosevelt famously stated, "No one cares how much you know until they know how much you care."[11] Those words were never truer than in International Church Planting.

Promote

It may sound overly obvious, but it is surprising how little most churches do to promote their presence in the public arena. I am constantly telling our leadership and our congregation that "the last thing we want to be is the best kept secret in the city!" The church is not like *The Field of Dreams*, where, "if you build it, they will come." The truth is, people will not come to a church simply because it exists. Think of how many businesses, even attractive, pleasant-looking businesses you pass by every day that you have never entered. We can't expect anyone to enter our church, small group or event unless we have let them know that <u>Who we are</u>, <u>What we are about</u>, <u>Where and When we meet</u>, <u>How to get there</u>, and <u>What to expect</u> when they arrive. Europe has a distinct advantage of having one of the most modern and complete communications systems on the planet. Virtually every form of media and communication device is available.

The internet is the most obvious first step – but it must not be taken for granted. A website is essential, and is the first way to "lay out the welcome mat" to your guests. Be sure that the mat is clean and attractive! Keep your website up to date. Nothing is more of a turn-off than bringing up a home page at Easter to find a church and find the Christmas schedule still on the home page! Find someone, or hire a service who will give you a professional and effective web

---

[11] Theodore Roosevelt. BrainyQuote.com, Xplore Inc, 2015. http://www.brainyquote.com/quotes/quotes/t/theodorero140484.html, accessed February 6, 2015.

presence. Find or hire a person to keep it updated at least weekly, and perhaps daily. You will find that nothing brings a better return on the investment than the money you put into your web presence.

Facebook has been our best and most consistent avenue of discovery. Look into facebook advertising. They give great control over the area you reach, the target demographics, and the amount you are willing to spend. We have found that a few dollars spent doing a saturation on facebook one week a month gives a great return. While it is widely reported that the young generations are steering away from it, we find that the people in our demographic are still firmly entrenched. Europe, Asia and Africa are perhaps not as quick to abandon facebook as the USA. That being said, it is wise to always keep your eyes and ears open when you are with your university students. Listen to their discussions. Ask questions. Find out where they are gathering on the web and be sure you are available there.

Explore other means of promotion. Be sure to have an attractive brochure with basic, well-presented information available at local hotels, student centers, dormitories and student housing centers. Go to multi-national corporations in your city and offer the personnel office for International transfers a pack of your brochures and business cards to be given in welcome packets for their new arrivals. Better yet – offer to provide the welcome packets if they are not doing one! Speaking of business cards – get them! Have a generic, two-sided card made up with the church name, location, times, web information and a small map. Leave room on the front for a member of your church to add their name and contact information. Distribute the cards to your members and encourage them to give them to every English-speaker they come across.

Is there an English-language theater in your city? Check with them about producing and placing a 30 second ad in the theater. Those coming to watch a movie in English are your target population – they are staring at the screen – why not let them know you are available for them? We found this to be a surprisingly affordable avenue of promotion – but, to be honest we were rather disappointed by the results. Try it for a few months at the most and see if you get results before continuing for any longer.

Billboards, posters, Bible distributions, signs and banners...the possibilities for promotion are only limited to your imagination and budget – be sure to include "advertising and promotion" in your budget from the very beginning – and don't stop! Remember, the average member is only going to be around for three years, so we need to keep identifying and reaching new people with the love of Christ.

Parent

From the earliest days of the church plant –plan to reproduce. A church that is committed to looking beyond its own survival, and toward the multiplication of the Kingdom of God, will be the kind of Church that brings an approving smile to the face of Jesus. At the launch service of Rome International Church in January of 2015, as they prepared to take up their first offering, Pastor Brian Kirby told the gathered crowd (many of whom were first time guests), "I want you to know that a portion of this offering, and every offering in the future, will be set aside for the planting of our next church in Rome!" THAT is how you get the idea into the DNA of the church from the very start!

We have had our eyes on a second church plant from before we arrived in Darmstadt. We are committed to seeing a second work – perhaps a satellite church – begun in either Heidelberg or Mannheim to the south of our current location. Both have large international communities, and both have recently suffered the loss of a number of English-language churches that were focused solely or primarily on the military community that has recently departed the area. There is a void that needs to be filled. With God's help we plan to meet that need!

Parenting can take many forms. It can be the beginning of a new church from another. It can also mean the participation of a church with several others in the support of a single work – with many churches sharing the effort and the joy of bringing for a new congregation. At the very least, church planters should be leading their church to actively and faithfully giving of their personal and financial resources to support church planting in their region.

Propel

One final item. We have mentioned a number of times the unique dynamic of International Churches – that we welcome and say goodbye with sometimes heart-rending regularity. Some have described this ministry as "ministering to a parade." We have adapted a core value as a church that we learned from Dr. Darryl Evetts, church planter of Frontline Community in Ramstein, Germany, and Director of Church Planting for the IBC. He shared early in our work together that they had decided to turn the tables on this often sad event. Instead of bemoaning the loss of a beloved member, we celebrate the commissioning of a new missionary! At Darmstadt we have adopted the core value "Lose None – Send All!" to summarize our view of God's work in this area.

When the time comes to bid farewell to a student who has completed their studies, or a business professional who is returning with their family to their home or perhaps advancing to another appointment, we bring them to the front of the church, we have the elders of the church, and those whom they have been closest with during their stay with us to come and we lay hands on them and commission them. Our theme verse for this part of our worship service is Acts 8:4, "Those who were scattered preached the word wherever they went."

May God lead each of us to plant and participate in churches that reach out to the lost, introduce them to Christ, mature them in the faith, and send them on mission – to His glory!

CHAPTER SIX
TRANSITIONING FROM MISSIONARY TO
INTERNATIONAL CHURCH PASTOR

By David Packer
Senior Pastor
International Baptist Church
Stuttgart, Germany

David Packer and his wife Lana served as missionaries to the Philippines, 1980-89, and as Senior Pastor and wife of the International Baptist Church (IBC) of Singapore, 1992-2004, of IBC Duesseldorf, Germany (2007-2009), and of IBC Stuttgart, Germany since 2009. In the USA he has been a youth minister, church planter, and senior pastor. He holds the Master of Divinity and the Doctor of Ministry from Southwestern Baptist Theological Seminary. They have three grown children and four grandchildren.

Under God's leadership, my wife, Lana, and I moved from being foreign missionaries to serving as pastor and wife of international churches overseas. We have served in three international churches: Singapore, Duesseldorf, and now Stuttgart.[12] This is the story of our own journey, or really my journey – I'll let Lana speak for herself. Although I am comparing the work of pastoring an international

---

[12] I recommend my book, *Look Who God Let into the Church*, the describes our experience in Singapore from 1992-2004. It is available online at amazon.com.

church and serving as a cross-cultural missionary, the differences, etc., I am not arguing that one is better than the other. All that matters is what God chooses us to do. Here is how He led us.

In 1980 God clarified for my wife and I our call to cross-cultural Christian work. We came to serve in the Philippines with the Philippine Baptist Mission under the auspices of the International Mission Board of the Southern Baptist Convention, USA. We were missionary's missionaries, committed to the work, learning the language, working cooperatively with the missionaries and with the Philippine churches, pastors, and national religious bodies.

We thought we would remain in the Philippines the rest of our missionary career and retire as missionaries to the Philippines. I became proficient in two Philippine languages (Cebuano and Tagalog) and we were completely involved as a family in the local churches. During our first furlough (home assignment) I completed the on-campus course work at Southwestern Baptist Theological Seminary for a Doctor of Ministry degree in World Missions. It was the furthest thing in our minds to do anything else.

During our second furlough, a serious illness with our daughter took us off of the mission field – due to a bad batch of measles vaccine, which she had received in the USA, the vaccination did not take and she came down with measles, also caught in the USA, which further developed into spinal meningitis and encephalitis. Her attending physician recommended that we do not return for at least two to three years overseas to a Third World tropical country, so we were suddenly left without an assignment. It was hard to shake the church planting identity and we turned down offers to pastor existing churches, opting to go to Austin, Texas, and start a church. After three years the church was doing fine and building its first church building, the Lord began to put world missions back on our hearts, and we started the process of praying about our next step. Because we had been off the foreign field for almost four years, and due to the fact that our oldest son was almost a teenager, the IMB wanted to carefully process us like first term missionaries, and made no promise on our re-appointment. We agreed that this was a good procedure as our children had become thoroughly Americanized during our time back to the USA.

During that time, however, we received an enquiry from the International Baptist Church of Singapore asking if we would be interested in serving as pastor and wife. During a few weeks of prayer and communication with the church we felt led to come and interview, and following our visit to the church they asked us to serve. We felt this matched our gifts and family situation perfectly, but, honestly, we had very little vision for international church work and thought we would be there for just a few years and then return to the Philippines or perhaps stay in Singapore in another role. Singapore is often called "Asia-lite" by missionaries, and it was definitely a softer reentry into Asia than returning to barrio evangelism in the Philippines. One thing that did warm my heart about pastoring IBC Singapore was the thought that we could help missionaries stay on the field by pastoring the church and offering their teenagers a good youth program.

Some have asked me if I left the IMB due to disagreements over theology or methodology. Let me clarify that neither of those matters played any role whatsoever. We were completely loyal Southern Baptists who had always been very supportive of its mission programs. The church we started in the USA and every church we had ever served with were at least ten percent Cooperative Program givers. So we found ourselves in a very strange condition – very loyal Southern Baptists and IMB supporters working alongside, but technically outside, of its organization.

The Differences

When Christ told Peter, "Feed my sheep" (John 21:17), it could be argued (and probably should be) that the work of pastoring is the generic nature of all ministry callings. To care for souls (Prov. 11:30), to build people up in their faith (2 Cor. 13:10), to encourage the maturity of others (Eph. 4:13), these indicate the concern of every

Christian, and certainly every called minister.

The one who is called to be the pastor-teacher of a church, who is responsible for teaching and preaching and soul-care, has the privilege of blessing others, of multiplying his faith through his teaching. Whatever else might be said about spiritual growth and discipleship, there can be no doubt that over the centuries the number one instrument that God has used for the spiritual growth of His people is the sermon. So the one who preaches plays an essential and significant role in the kingdom of God.

One of the key differences between pastoring and being a missionary is just this: that I was responsible for the spiritual development of people in my church including missionaries. So though my work was related to preaching rather than going out and starting churches, it was still about multiplication of the gospel through making spiritual investments in the lives of the people who came and worshiped.

Gradually I began to realize several other differences between my work as a pastor of an international church and the role of missionaries. Here is a partial list.

First, I realized as a pastor that I was working in specific, direct ways and they, the missionaries, were working in more indirect ways. My work was very dependent on the growth and health of one church, and their work was more general and even somewhat vague in terms of results. I was the senior pastor, so I was the servant-leader of the church staff, and missionaries serve more as colleagues alongside of one another without one being directly over another (there are exceptions to this, of course). They normally had opportunities for lateral moves to other jobs within the mission, and I was specifically connected to only one church.

Secondly, missionaries work with one or two cultures, and I was working with several. They were seeking to become connected to one cultural ministry, and I was dealing with how to lead people from many different nations toward a common goal. This led to my awareness that there was an element within Singapore that was truly multi-cultural, that the local churches were not reaching, or even acknowledging. And this segment of population included many Singaporeans, as well as internationals.

Thirdly, they were working more with the leaders of the churches, and we were working with everybody in the church. In fact, we spent more time ministering to the troubled people than we did dealing with the church leaders. We counseled people for numerous needs, performed marriages, did pre-marital and marital counseling, led Bible studies, led services, witnessed in homes, led children to Christ, etc. – the normal pastor things. The things I was busy with were preparing sermons, leading staff meetings, counseling, leading meetings, training workers, and did I say counseling? We were busy dealing with normal people and their normal problems.

I found myself more connected in intimate ways with local people, and people from around the world, than I did as a missionary. As a missionary I spent time with the local people in the Philippines, became close to many of them, learned their culture and their language, but I was not their pastor, and encouraged them to go to their pastors for spiritual nourishment. Yet our experience in Singapore as pastor and wife was extremely close and personal in terms of dealing with people. Many missionaries have a broad, text-book, but somewhat vague view and understanding of the local cultures in which they serve. Missionary promotions to positions of leadership in the mission can often come on the basis of how well one relates to his fellow missionaries, and not how well he relates to the local people. Our work was close-up, personal, and intimate.

This difference was highlighted when Lana was sharing with a long-serving missionary wife about the many married couples we were counseling. Lana commented on how common the problem of adultery is in Christian marriages, to which the missionary replied that she thought that only happened in International Baptist Church, and not in the other Singaporean churches – she and her husband had served for over thirty years in Singapore. I am convinced that she was out of touch with the reality of Singaporean churches, but in truth she was dealing almost exclusively with the leadership of the churches. She knew very few normal Christians in Singapore.

Fourthly, we dealt with the week-to-week, Sunday-to-Sunday, and even the year-to-year reality of the church program and were very busy. Missionaries work hard – I know because I served with them and as one of them – but I believe pastors work harder. Sunday comes around each week and a new sermon must be prepared, things must get done, staff issues must be resolved. As anyone who has served knows, there is a grind and a routine to pastoring a church. It is harder to find time to get away and re-charge your spiritual and emotional batteries. A missionary can have a home assignment (or furlough) and turn his work over to a colleague for a few months or longer, but a pastor is much less able to have that kind of flexibility.

Fifthly, the financial differences: I discovered that most missionaries are not aware of the actual cost of their ministry. Many raise part of their support, but rarely do they raise all. The IMB, as a denominational mission agency pays all of the support for its missionaries. Due to this, such matters as home leave, airfare, children's education, automobiles, health insurance, retirement, convention or conference allowances, financial adjustments due to currency exchanges, substitute preachers, etc., are not always thought of.

Whereas for me it was all amazingly clear. The church paid for everything and I was ultimately directly responsible for raising the support money for myself and the staff from the attendees and members of the church. My supporters were not on another continent blissfully unaware of what I did or what I did not do. They saw me every Sunday.

Sixthly, and finally, as pastor of one church my field to evangelize was specific and somewhat limited. Missionaries plow larger ground for Christ and this is one of the real thrilling privileges of missionary service. However, if they run into a problem, or face rejection, they are able to move to some other place to work. As pastor, however, I dealt primarily with only one church in one city, a limited and specific list of people, with no place else to go and serve that did not involve a complete change in jobs, ministries, pay checks, health insurance, employee policies, etc.

Servanthood and Usefulness

I believe servanthood is an essential attitude for effective ministry in any situation. In cross-cultural missions it means that we listen to our national brothers and sisters, and make ourselves available for them to meet the needs they feel they have, that we do not try to lord it over them, but humbly seek to come alongside and help – to learn as well as lead. I have learned much from my Singaporean, Philippine, and German fellow pastors and church leaders. I have been blessed by listening to their advice, just as hopefully I have been a blessing to them. I do not doubt, however, that I have received more than I have given.

Leadership for missionaries tends to have a more withdrawn and indirect nature about it. Missionaries will commonly say that they are trying to work themselves out of a job, and, especially since the emphasis of such missiologists as Roland Allen, and the Indigenous Church Movement, they are focused on letting the national church leaders make the key decisions. As the senior pastor, however, I was directly involved in matters in the church, and could not and should not defer to others to make some key decisions. I had to know what were the best solutions to specific problems, and had to work with leadership to achieve real progress.

Decisions that churches make also generally have more lay involvement in them than those that missionaries make. Missionaries may have access to the latest studies, demographic trends, unreached people groups, and theories of mission work. They will often have time for reflection and consultations by the best experts in the field. Good missionaries read a lot and are typically very knowledgeable about mission work. But for pastors and for churches, decisions are more likely to be made in the heat of the moment, when someone knows someone who knows someone, or people have some work on their heart. Decisions in a church have more input by average lay people, and less by the "experts." People in churches tend to want to support a certain work because it touches their heart in some fashion, not because it is strategically viable.

Somewhat to my surprise, I found that we began receiving many invitations from Christian leaders in the entire Southeast Asia region to serve in different ways. We had less time to help other churches, but we came to help with a track record in ministry that recommended us to them, and in some ways we felt we were more effective. By the time we left Singapore, we had done mission work in ten other Asian nations. Pastors want to know what other pastors are doing that is working. The most helpful and practical advice in any field always comes from those who are involved in the work themselves.

When I served as a missionary I taught seminary courses or preached in churches and I felt I was very effective, well-respected, and appreciated. But I was really usually presenting material that someone else had developed. As pastor of a large and continually growing church in Singapore I found that people wanted to know what I was doing. I once spoke for the Malaysian Baptist Convention, and following the meeting a missionary told me that he had no idea why they asked me, since I was relatively new to the area – and he had served there almost 40 years.

I am not being critical of the missionary – he really was a good, sacrificial servant – but to me as a pastor it was very clear why they had asked me. I was directly involved in the work, and the growth of the missionary's work, as important as it was, was less clear. I was pastoring a church in Southeast Asia. I was a practitioner not a theorist. My advice came not in the form of theory or the latest book I read, but from the life and ministry of an active pastor. I was unencumbered by mission organization policies, and my church and

I could do what we felt the Lord was calling us to do. And I am not critical of mission organizations – in fact, we financially supported many missionaries while I was pastor. But I found that my role as pastor was not exactly the same as that as a missionary.

Not all that I did was different from missionaries. We were still in our forties when we arrived and the bulk of the IMB missionaries were nearing retirement or had already retired, and there was no plan to replace them. The feeling of the IMB leadership was that they had accomplished their job and would assign new missionaries to unreached peoples. In that situation, many roles that missionaries had filled came to me, and I was able to serve on committees on the Singapore Baptist Convention, and to teach as an adjunct lecturer at Baptist Theological Seminary in Singapore. Though the Baptist leaders were quite capable of standing on their own, our presence there let them know that they were not forgotten. We were privileged to serve as a bit of a buffer between the end of the missionary era to the beginning of the independent Singaporean church leader era.

I also noticed that the missionaries tended to be committed to some programs that had been begun in the past, whether they were effective or not. Their loyalty was sometimes admirable, but also sometimes relatively fruitless, and we could not afford the luxury of failure. So we looked for what was working, what God was blessing, and not what had the mission committed to doing twenty years earlier.

Making the Transition into a New Role

In spite of the sense of calling to this new role, I did find it more difficult than I had expected to make the transition, and I experience a real sense of loss. First, there was very little involvement in worldwide mission issues – I especially felt this loss since my doctorate was in World Missions. I was somewhat out of touch with an area of information that was very important to me personally. Singapore is a great place to study missions, and the Christians in the city often speak of themselves as the Antioch of the East, so it was not a complete blackout of information, but I did miss the connections and the ongoing flow of information, new studies, movements of the Spirit, etc.

Second, there was also the loss of the mission family. We had been very connected with the International Mission Board and with Southern Baptists, so we did feel the loss of not having this large and loving missionary family to support us, even though we did have many close personal friends in Singapore. Due to a personnel conflict in the Singapore Mission, which eventually led to the dismissal of a missionary, we withdrew from the mission fellowship to allow the missionaries to work these details out. I wrote adult Bible studies for Lifeway Christian Resources for several years, and quite often I wrote the December world mission emphasis even though I personally received no benefit from it. As the church was very fair with my salary I did not need the money, but we did miss the connection with the greater mission family.

Over the years I was there I would sometimes receive contact from a church in the USA asking if I was interested in serving as their pastor. We felt our obligation was normally to sincerely pray through these invitations. Inevitably the question would come up, "Are you a missionary or a pastor?" And sometimes even I was not sure how to answer it. Gradually I realized that God was doing what He had often done through the centuries. He was turning us into an international couple to minister in a world that is also becoming quite international itself. We changed and became different people, much more grounded in the local work and bonded to the local people, as well as to the international people who came and went.

Sometimes I hear someone say something like, "You can reach the whole world through the international church." That is a romantic idea, but I do not believe this is a realistic statement. The international church is a niche market for Christ that meets a need of a certain part of the world's population. It is a neglected part that has great potential, and I believe it was a lack of understanding and vision for the International Mission Board to pull out of helping these churches. Some places, especially in Europe, there is a great need for international churches. The "Homogenous Unit" methodology is not an absolute truth, yet the international church is not for everyone, nor can you reach the majority people of the world through international churches.

Missionaries affirm one another as they become more like the nationals. The goal of missionaries is to bond with the local culture, to learn the language and the ways of the local churches and Christians if there are some, and, if not, to start a Christian movement in that culture. Pastors of international churches may feel that their responsibility is to remain bonded to their home culture, and to have a church that is an enclave of American or Western culture (or Korean, Chinese, etc.). If international churches will reach their potential they will also reach out compassionately to the local population. If they will reach their potential, the pastors and leaders must make the painful but essential transition from being cultural citizens of only one nation, to becoming true internationals themselves – conversant in more than one language, comfortable in more than one culture, effective and competent to preach and counsel in a variety of cultures – the more the better.

A few years ago at a meeting of the international church pastors, the difference between international pastors and cross-cultural missionaries became very clear. At the hotel breakfast buffet I put fish on my plate. Having spent most of our lives outside the USA both my wife and I like fish for breakfast – very common in Southeast Asia, but not so common in America. Before I could sit down two American pastors at the same hotel buffet felt obliged to make negative comments about my eating fish for breakfast. They said this somewhat in jest, but the fact that they noticed what I put on my plate, and that they thought it was a good idea to send some friendly chastisement my way said something. This was an action of rather benign "cultural imperialism" and the pastors took on the role of cultural enforcers, determined to make sure I knew that Americans did not eat fish for breakfast.

It was said in jest, but it also revealed that pastors of international churches could see other cultures negatively, rather than positively. They may feel their job is to build churches that "do it right" rather than to join the worldwide movement of God that involves all cultures. One of the first requirements to have any influence with people from other cultures is to "accept the acceptable" in their culture with out passing judgment. Certainly fish for breakfast is one of these "acceptables." To try to negatively enforce cultural cohesiveness by rejecting acculturation is common among immigrants, but it is not the way to build a worldwide international multicultural Christian movement.

So, in some minor ways, I still feel myself somewhat at odds with many of my fellow pastors of international churches. I love and appreciate them, but feel they are not all well-trained in understanding the importance of acculturation and respect of people from other cultures and societies. The adage is: "We go where we are celebrated, not where we are tolerated." We need to do more than tolerate people different from us. We need to celebrate them.

But in more important ways, I feel myself very much bonded to the pastors of international churches because they, like me, are directly involved in the work. They are not theorists; rather they are practitioners of the work of cross-cultural ministry. So I have gradually made the adjustment to appreciate these men and women who serve in a variety of capacities to strengthen, grow, and build up these international churches around the globe.

A surprising serendipity is the privilege of serving as a direct example to other local pastors. It is impossible to do meaningful Christian work if all the witnesses are mere theorists – some must be practitioners who model Christian ministry and spiritual servanthood. I understand very well the history behind the decision and why so many mission agencies moved their missionaries out of the role of serving as pastors, and into the roles of encouragers and equippers of native pastors – they were slowing down the expansion of the churches by holding positions that local indigenous people could do. When the missionaries were removed from serving as pastors of the churches, this has usually led to a greater expansion of the churches through the elevation of the native pastors themselves.

However, I have often wondered if we gave up too much with this concession. I have wondered how the words of Paul would have ever had real power and meaning if that was the method of the First Century: "Whatever you have learned or received or heard from me, or seen in me—put it into practice" (Phil. 4:9). How can any real ministry be effectively transplanted without some serving as models of ministry, and especially models of the work of the pastor?

Even a simple look at the church of Jesus Christ worldwide, taking in the broad sweep of church history, confronts us with the impact of the pastor and the preacher. The effectiveness of the church in ministry and outreach depends absolutely, both in the short run and in the long run, on this position of pastor-teacher being effectively filled, the heart of which is soul care, spiritual leadership, and proclamation. I question whether the move away from missionaries pastoring, the strict move to indigenous churches, was wise in every circumstance. So, as an international church pastor, as imperfectly as I fill this role and do this work, I feel effective in a way that my missions training did not prepare me for, but which I have learned is essential for the success and growth of the church – the direct modeling of pastoring and preaching to people from different cultures.

CHAPTER SEVEN
GLOBAL NOMADS: EXPATS ON MISSION IN A NEW URBAN WORLD[13]

By Jacob Bloemberg
Hanoi International Fellowship
Hanoi, Vietnam

Jacob Bloemberg is Lead Pastor at the Hanoi International Fellowship (www.hif.vn) in the capital city of Vietnam. He and his wife Linda have served in Hanoi since 1997, where they have raised three children. A Dutch citizen with an American wife, they have learned to thrive in a third culture and aim to help others thrive as well. Jacob is ordained and sent by Elim Fellowship, NY. With an MA in Organizational Leadership from Regent University, Jacob is on his journey to finish the Doctorate in Transformational Leadership program with a focus on City Transformation through Bakke Graduate University. Jacob serves on the leadership team of the Missional International Church Network (www.micn.org) and implements the missional vision with HIF through the Love Hanoi campaign (www.lovehanoi.org).

International churches are uniquely positioned to be strategically engaged in urban mission in any given context. With a wealth of

---

[13] Originally printed in: Graham Hill (Ed.). *Signs of Hope in the City: Renewing Urban Mission, Embracing Radical Hope*. Melbourne: UNOH, 2015. Used with permission.

resources, know-how, and well connected people, they can have a huge impact within their cities. Sadly, international churches are often perceived as Christian clubs for expatriates with little relevancy to the community in which they are located. It is true, many do start that way, but that is not the ideal nor should they stay that way.

In this chapter, I will start off by showing how the first missional movement led by the Apostle Paul was birthed in an international church and continued to plant such churches through the Western world. In addition, research has proven that, though much history has been lost, the church thrived in urban centres throughout the Eastern and Southern hemispheres. The global diaspora of people during those early centuries paved the way.

Such a diaspora movement is happening in our century as well. Several networks are envisioning this trend to be an opportunity for ministry to, through, and beyond the diaspora. This is where and how international churches today can be most effective, by mobilizing today's global nomads for urban mission. I will briefly talk about the role of international churches, affluent churches, and pastors in citywide movements.

It is important for international churches to understand their own urban context in order to contextualize urban ministry. A short discussion of contextualization is presented and illustrated by my own context, the city of Hanoi, Vietnam. Moving forward, I will describe how partnerships and networking are vital for international churches to launch citywide movements to love their cities. Using the Love Hanoi campaign as an example, I will explain the first stages of starting a movement. Because, if we can do it in Hanoi, other international churches around the world certainly can too!

1. Biblical and Historical Precedence

The involvement of the international church in citywide movements and global urban mission is not a new endeavour. In fact, there are both biblical and historical precedents from the first century and the first millennium that are repeating it today. To begin with, let me take you back to the sending church of the Apostle Paul. I will then take you across the Asian continent and back to Africa to show how the early church thrived in urban centres of ancient Christian, Muslim, and Buddhist nations.

Antioch: The First Missional International Church

"Now those who had been scattered by the persecution that broke out when Stephen was killed," it says in Acts chapter eleven, "travelled as far as Phoenicia, Cyprus, and Antioch, spreading the word only among Jews. Some of them, however, men from Cyprus and Cyrene, went to Antioch and began to speak to Greeks also, telling them the good news about the Lord Jesus".[14] Although churches had been planted in Jerusalem, Judea, and Samaria, this was the first time disciples of Jesus were venturing outside their national borders towards the ends of the earth. Not by choice, mind you, but some shared the gospel with non-Jews and soon enough the first congregation outside Israel was born. It became so successful that Luke writes, "The Lord's hand was with them, and a great number of people believed and turned to the Lord".[15] For a whole year, "Barnabas and Saul met with the church and taught great numbers of people".[16] The Antioch church was a large, non-Jewish, urban church.

When a visiting prophet came from Jerusalem and foretold about the upcoming famine in Israel, the Christians (for they were first called Christians in Antioch) started sending money down to help the poor. The Antioch church was a missional church. Two chapters later, Luke records the leadership team of the Antioch church gathering for a conference. He relays those who were present: "Barnabas, Simeon called Niger, Lucius of Cyrene, Manaen (who had been brought up with Herod the tetrarch) and Saul".[17] Each of these men came from a

---

[14] Acts 11:19-20 NIV.
[15] Acts 11:21 NIV.
[16] Acts 11:26 NIV.
[17] Act 13:1 NIV.

different nationality. The Antioch church was an international church. In response to the word from the Holy Spirit, the leadership team set aside Barnabas and Paul and sent them off on the first international mission journey. The Antioch church was a sending church.

The First-Century Diaspora: Global Urban Missional Movement

The church in Antioch was truly remarkable: it was a large, non-Jewish, urban, missional, international, and sending church with great sensitivity to the move of the Holy Spirit. As a result, the Antioch church became a launching pad for a global urban missional movement that is still going on today. It became a model church for all the churches Paul, Barnabas, and their teammates planted throughout the Roman empire. The Antioch church is still a model church for us today.

Within a time span of 25 years, this missional movement had spread from Antioch throughout Asia Minor across to the European continent and as far as Rome, the empire's capital city. This was made possible because of the first-century diaspora of the Jewish people. Since the days of the exile, Jews had settled in cities throughout the Assyrian empire and established synagogues wherever they lived. Only ten men were needed to start a synagogue, though some newer cities like Philippi did not even have that many. Paul and his international church-planting team traversed from city to city — it was an urban missional strategy. The Roman empire had paved the way, literally. In part due to the transportation infrastructure, a common language, and the diaspora network, Paul's mission was a success.

From Antioch to the Far East and Back

Not only was Antioch the launching pad for the Western (Roman) church, but also for the Eastern (Asian) church. It is a popular, though erroneous, belief that after Paul's mission, the gospel kept moving west into Europe, then the USA, then to Asia, and is now making its way back to Jerusalem. However, during the first thousand-year history of the church, it was predominantly an Asian church.

In *The Lost History of Christianity: The Thousand-Year Golden Age of the Church in the Middle East, Africa, and Asia — and How It Died*, Philip Jenkins uncovers the forgotten roots of the Asian church. Long before the Roman Catholics travelled The Silk Road to China, the Nestorian and Jacobite missionaries set out from Syria to the Far East, reaching as far as Mongolia, Shanghai, India, and perhaps as far as Vietnam, the Philippines, and Korea.[18] It is estimated that by the year 1000AD, "Asia had 17 to 20 million Christians" who "stemmed from Christian traditions dating back twenty-five or thirty generations".[19]

Nestorians in the seventh century had contextualized the gospel in such a way that they were able to communicate it in Buddhist and Taoist terms. Here is a sample text from a Nestorian monument dating back to 780AD:

> "The illustrious and honourable Messiah, veiling his true dignity, appeared in the world as a man; ... he fixed the extent of the eight boundaries, thus completing the truth and freeing it from dross; he opened the gate of the three constant principles, introducing life and destroying death; he suspended the bright sun to invade the chambers of darkness, and the falsehoods of the devil were thereupon defeated; he set in motion the vessel of mercy by which to ascend to the bright mansions, whereupon rational beings were then released; having thus completed the manifestation of his power, in clear day he ascended to his true station."[20]

Another example is the design used by the Nestorians to identify

---

[18] Philip Jenkins, *The Lost History of Christianity: The Thousand-Year Golden Age of the Church in the Middle East, Africa, and Asia — and How It Died*, 1st ed. (New York: HarperOne, 2008), 70.
[19] Ibid., 70.
[20] Jenkins, 15.

themselves, namely a cross on top of a lotus, the "symbol of Buddhist enlightenment".[21] This symbol can be found even today on tombstones throughout China and India. The image below depicts the icon found on a tombstone in China (see Figure 1: Headstone with Lotus and Cross, Yuan Dynasty (1272–1368), Quanzhou Maritime Museum). This symbol is an inspiring example for Asian Christian designers today. For the past two thousand years, Christian artists have been designing church logos or symbols. Designers today are continuing an ancient trade of applying contextualization to their art. What would a contextualized church logo in Asia look like today?

Figure 1: Headstone with Lotus and Cross, Yuan Dynasty (1272–1368), Quanzhou Maritime Museum[22]

As the title of Jenkins' book suggests, much of the church's history in Asia, the Middle East, and Africa has been lost. Yet, what is known is that at the start of the third century several kingdoms were Christian in religion. The king of Osthoene, with Edessa as its capital city,

---

[21] Ibid.

[22] USF Ricci Institute, "The Lotus and the Cross: East-West Cultural Exchange along the Silk Road," University of San Francisco (accessed 4 June 2014).

accepted Christianity around 200AD.[23] Armenia followed around 300AD, of which the capital city Ani became known as "the city of 1,001 churches".[24] Next in line were Georgia, Adiabene, Nubida, and Ethiopia (Abyssinia). Aksum, Ethiopia's capital, became "the kingdom's main Christian see" by 340AD.[25] Ethiopia was so full of churches that it was said one could not "sing in one church without being heard by another, and perhaps by several". Furthermore, the Christians had "a natural disposition to goodness, they [were] very liberal of their alms".[26]

Much of the non-Western church history might have been lost, but Jenkins has proven that Christianity thrived in urban centres and numerous nations during the first millennium. The church, to begin with, was urban and Asian.

2. The Missional International Church Movement of Today

Having established that the church of Acts was a missional movement of international churches which continued to thrive in urban centres of the East, South, and West, we will now jump ahead to the third millennium in which we find ourselves. First, we will briefly highlight current trends of the global diaspora and the Global Diaspora Network. Then, the Missional International Church Network and, as an example, the Hanoi International Fellowship, will be introduced to show how international churches today can play an effective role in urban mission. Considering the wealth of resources in such churches, attention is given to the role of international churches, the affluent, and the pastor.

The Twenty-First-Century Global Diaspora

Akin to the first-century diaspora, the global dispersion of people today is an unprecedented flow of people migrating predominantly from East to West, South to North, and rural to urban environments.

---

[23] Jenkins, 54.
[24] Ibid.
[25] Ibid., 55.
[26] Ibid., 56.

According to the Global Diaspora Network (GDN), "there are now over 200 million international migrants, and over 700 million internally displaced people or close to 1 billion scattered peoples".[27] To visualize this global movement, the Wittgenstein Centre for Demography and Global Human Capital has done a beautiful job creating an information graph as shown in Figure 2. It is worthwhile to go to the website www.global-migration.info and download the high resolution PDF data sheets. I had these printed on banners and posted them at our church to raise awareness of this global trend.

Migration flows within and between ten world regions, in 100,000s. This circular plot shows all global bilateral migration flows for the five-year period mid-2005 to mid-2010, classified into a manageable set of ten world regions. Key features of the global migration system include the high concentration of African migration within the continent (with the exception of Northern Africa), the "closed" migration system of the former Soviet Union, and the high spatial focus of Asian emigration to North America and the Gulf states.

Cities are the places where these streams of global migration merge. In these urban centres of globalization, migration, and urbanization is where international churches (ICs) thrive. In every major city around the world there are ICs which serve the dynamic expatriate community. Generally, expatriates roam the world like global nomads from city to city, job to job, posting to posting, and calling to calling. It is like a rushing river streaming around the globe. Among them are Christians from all kinds of nationalities, vocations, and denominations. The Missional International Church Network (MICN)[28] is focused on mobilizing ICs to empower this global stream of Christian expats to be missional wherever they go.

[27] Sadiri Joy Tira, ed. *The Human Tidal Wave* (Pasig City, Philippines: Lifechange Publishing, Inc., 2013), xxi.
[28] Visit www.micn.org for more information.

Figure 2: The Global Flow of People[29]

One of these ICs is the Hanoi International Fellowship (HIF), which I have the privilege to serve as Lead Pastor. HIF started as a fellowship of about a dozen Christian expats in the capital city of Vietnam some 20 years ago. For the first decade, the fellowship was internally focused, primarily meeting the needs of Christian foreigners living and working in Hanoi. In 2005, just before my appointment as the pastor, I attended the MICN conference, which was held in Dubai that year. As a church we had come to realize that God was calling us to

---

[29] Nikola Sander, Guy Abel, and Ramon Bauer, "The Global Flow of People," Wittgenstein Centre for Demography and Global Human Capital http://www.global-migration.info/ (accessed 29 March 2014).

become externally focused, but how could we do this as an IC in our context? MICN provided us with a vision, language, and peer group which helped HIF to transform into a missional community.

The Role of the International Church

Joy Tira, director of Global Diaspora Network (GDN), calls upon the church to respond to the global diaspora phenomenon. Tira outlines three ways for Christians and churches to get involved, by ministering *to*, *through*, and *beyond* the diaspora.[30] This provides a helpful framework to categorize the types of ministries the IC can be involved with. For example, by reaching out to the expatriate community in Hanoi, HIF is ministering directly *to* the diaspora in our city. Mobilizing and equipping HIF members to be missional is ministering *through* the diaspora. When HIFers become acquainted with the culture and context, we are able to minister *beyond* the diaspora and build bridges with local communities and society. International churches are uniquely positioned to become bridge builders between the global diaspora and the local population, between the global church and the local congregations, and between global organizations and corporations to meet local needs.

One of the challenges that I continued to struggle with is this: how can an international church transition from being a church that has come "to" the city, to being a church that is "in" the city, to being a church that is "for" the city, to becoming a church that collaborates "with" the city? Hanoi International Fellowship transitioned some years ago from being a fellowship of Christian foreigners to becoming a missional international church. We have come to realize that we are called to be a city church, a church that is "in" and "for" the city. Today, the challenge before us is the next transition: to become a church that is *with* the city. How can HIF collaborate across sectors and with city institutions to be a blessing to the city of Hanoi? Or, in the words of Swanson and Williams, how can the *whole* church

---

[30] Tira, ed., 163.

bring the *whole* gospel to the *whole* city?[31]

The Role of the Affluent Church

Equipping expatriate Christians to serve the poor in the city immediately raises the issue: how can the affluent expats help without hurting? Lowell Bakke, professor at the Bakke Graduate University (BGU), stated during a lecture on urban transformation: "The boulevard churches speak to power; the off-street churches speak to people".[32] This means that there is room for both the upscale downtown church as well as the neighbourhood community churches.

During my study in Manila for a BGU course, I had a chance to visit two boulevard churches (Union Church Manila, a one-hundred-year old international church, and Christ Commission Fellowship, a local wealthy church with a brand-new, debt-free, 10,000-seat facility) and two off-street churches (Botocan Christian Community Fellowship in a squatter area and the small church in the Wawa slum community). I know that most members of the international church cannot do what the people in the squatter community churches are doing. However, the opposite is also true: the small house churches cannot influence those in positions of power in the city and nation. What is important is that both the affluent and the community churches work on behalf of the poor.

While reading and researching about urban ministry, I fell into the trap of believing that, unless you move into the poor neighbourhood and live like the poor, you cannot effectively help the poor. Incarnational ministry, as it is often labelled, can be easily misunderstood as being at the pinnacle of the ministry pyramid (see Figure 3).

In the evangelical church exists a mindset that it is more holy to

---

[31] Eric Swanson and Sam Williams, *To Transform a City: Whole Church, Whole Gospel, Whole City* (Grand Rapids, MI: Zondervan, 2010).
[32] Lowell Bakke, "Introduction," in *Overture 1: Manila* (Manila, Philippines: Bakke Graduate University, 2014).

serve God as an evangelist, pastor, or missionary than it is to have any other job. This view is very much prevalent among Asian churches. The saying is, "If you really want to serve God, quit your job and work for him full-time". This is a false mindset, since every Christian is called to serve God in their homes, offices, classrooms, neighbourhoods, and wherever else they work, live, and go. The danger is that incarnational ministry is viewed as the most sacred and effective way — perhaps the only way — to serve the poor in the city.

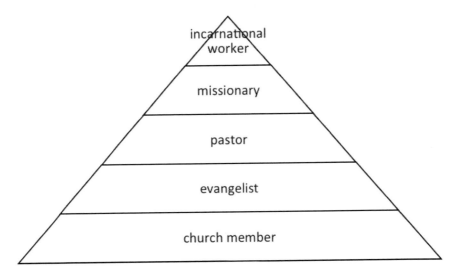

Figure 3: The Ministry Pyramid

It is true that incarnational ministry can be very effective if done well. Viv Grigg, founder of Servant Partners, has mobilized many incarnational workers and missionaries who have laid down their riches to live and serve among the poor in slums around the world. Aaron Smith, whom I met in the Botocan squatter community, is one of them. However, it is apparent that only few are called to such extremes and often for a relatively short time. What about the rest of the church? Can they serve the poor besides supporting the incarnational missionaries? If incarnational ministry is seen as the pinnacle of mission, everyone else will always feel like their service is of lesser value — that they will never measure up or can help effectively.

Thankfully, Grigg offers a much broader picture. He writes, "Typical Christian responses of aid and community development, even when done brilliantly, affect only the micro-environment of the squatter area".[33] Grigg goes on to explain that there is a distinct role for the affluent Christian:

"The primary response of middle-class Christians (while not neglecting other issues) will probably be in the transformation of economic life, political life, government bureaucracy, and other structures of the city that perpetuate slum poverty. It will probably also be necessary to deal with international factors that increasingly loom as dominant forces in worldwide urban poverty."[34]

In chapters 20 and 21 of his book, *Cry of the Urban Poor*, Grigg offers his recommendations for middle-class and international elite Christians and churches. "Middle-class professionals ... may effect change in the implementation and governing of the cities at an urban planning level," while "Christians in the international elite may change the macro-economic systems".[35] Table 1 below outlines potential responses of the middle-class to poverty.

In speaking of the role of the affluent church, Grigg states, "Far more important [than giving financial help] is giving personnel who can impart spiritual life and technical skills".[36] Still, it is valid to provide financial support for widows, orphans, refugees, seed capital, expansion capital, scholarships, and community leadership programs.[37] Figure 4 charts out what the upper and middle classes can do in the fight against poverty.

Figure 5 displays how a simplified lifestyle of Westerners (or the

---

[33] Viv Grigg, *Cry of the Urban Poor* (Monrovia, Calif.: MARC, 1992), 262.
[34] Viv Grigg, *Cry of the Urban Poor* (Monrovia, Calif.: MARC, 1992), 263.
[35] Ibid.
[36] Grigg, 283.
[37] Grigg, 283-284.

affluent) can lift the labouring poor of developing nations out of poverty, which in turn lifts the destitute poor up to becoming the labouring poor.

Table 1: Middle-Class Responses to Poverty

LEVELS OF POVERTY	POTENTIAL RESPONSES
Street sleepers	Social work relating to existing agencies Direct aid — food, clothing Food for work, housing
Relocation area	Upgrade work operations Food for work or housing Social work relating to existing agencies
Bustees/Slums (Where housing available, no work)	Co-op loans draw local industries into area Co-op into job placement, feasibility studies of jobs Direct grants to establish small-scale businesses: Food line Clothing line Manufacturing line: Electronics Welding Woodworking Chemicals, soaps Avoid handicrafts unless there are existing skills A skills-training institution nearby Food for work Overseas job placement agency
Slum-housed (Majority working)	Co-op housing program Credit co-op
Drug addicts, alcoholics	Specialized long-term pastoral communities and rehabilitation

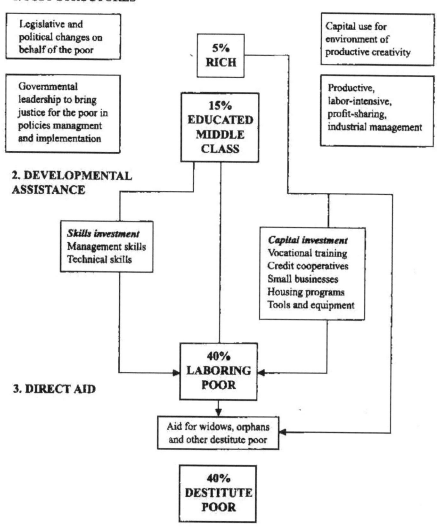

1. JUST STRUCTURES

Legislative and political changes on behalf of the poor

Governmental leadership to bring justice for the poor in policies managment and implementation

Capital use for environment of productive creativity

Productive, labor-intensive, profit-sharing, industrial management

5% RICH

15% EDUCATED MIDDLE CLASS

2. DEVELOPMENTAL ASSISTANCE

Skills investment
Management skills
Technical skills

Capital investment
Vocational training
Credit cooperatives
Small businesses
Housing programs
Tools and equipment

3. DIRECT AID

40% LABORING POOR

Aid for widows, orphans and other destitute poor

40% DESTITUTE POOR

Aim: To transfer skills, technology, tools, and control of capital to the productive poor.

Figure 4: The Fight against Poverty: What the upper and middle class can do[38]

---

[38] Grigg, 285.

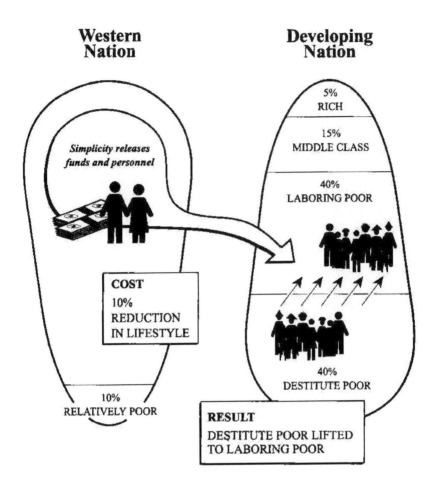

Western Nation

Simplicity releases funds and personnel

COST
10%
REDUCTION
IN LIFESTYLE

10%
RELATIVELY POOR

Developing Nation

5%
RICH

15%
MIDDLE CLASS

40%
LABORING POOR

40%
DESTITUTE POOR

RESULT
DESTITUTE POOR LIFTED
TO LABORING POOR

REMOVING BARRIERS
Migration barriers
Multinational controls
Usurious interest
internationally

CREATING OPPORTUNITIES
Financing credit coop.
Scholarships for vocational training
Transfer of tools and equipment
Transfer of technical knowledge
Transfer of skilled personnel

Figure 5: Sacrificial, Simple Lifestyles: Interchurch international economic justice (2 Corinthians 8–9)[39]

At HIF, we are moving in the direction Grigg is pointing through our City Partnerships ministry. It is our aim to connect resources in HIF

---

[39] Grigg, 286.

with opportunities in the city. We recruit volunteers to share their time and expertise, and to raise funds to support initiatives such as orphanages, vocational projects, and start-up ministries. The vision, guidelines, and implementation of City Partnerships need clarification and refinement. It would help our middle-class and international, elite church members to clearly see their individual role in fighting poverty as well as our corporate role in the city.

The challenge of reducing our lifestyle by 10% in order to uplift the productive poor could be turned into a campaign for financial stewardship. The campaign could challenge HIF members to live on 80% of their income, while giving 10% to ministries and 10% to the church.

The Role of the Pastor

To overcome these challenges, one change that needs to take place is in the pastor's posture towards the city. Is he or she the "pastor in a church which *happens to be in* a community or which is *for* a community?" questions Lowell Bakke. The answer to this question unveils what the pastor thinks about their role in the city. During my tenure as pastor of HIF, I also needed to make this paradigm shift. When we decided to be a church *for* the expatriate community and *for* the city, it changed my role and posture as well. The city had become my parish.

During one of our lectures in Manila, Raineer Chu, attorney with Mission Ministries Philippines (MMP), challenged us to consider the posture of the Catholic priest. "Learn to journey with the poor, all other things become secondary," said Chu. In coming to a community, the comparison between a Catholic priest and an evangelical pastor provides quite a contrast in posture. Chu explained:

> "When entering the slum, a priest has a very graphic image of Jesus (as a statue) whereas a pastor has the image of Jesus' presence (ethereal). A priest has a theology of God's presence everywhere. A priest comes to the community to find God there

whereas the pastor goes to bring God. The priest in his order goes there to grow old there, die there, and be buried there. Francis Schaeffer, in his books, says evangelicals have already "found" Jesus whereas the orthodox have a great sense of journey. Pastors divide between members and non-members; the priest is called to the parish."[40]

The table below lists the differing postures between priest and pastor (see Table 2). Obviously, this is exaggerated and stereotyping, but it worked on me. Looking at the pastor column, I can identify more with the pastor than the priest: bringing God to the city, focused on accomplishing a project, moving fast, and a focus on preaching and communication. Now I have a dilemma: I want to see the city as my parish, but I have to fight against my default approach to the city as a typical pastor.[41]

Table 2: Contrast between the Priest and Pastor [42]

PRIEST	PASTOR
Theology of finding God	Bringing God
Journey	Project accomplished
Walk slowly	Walks fast
Called to entire parish	Divide members/non-members
Focus on sick, poor, dying	Focus on Scripture

One excellent example of such a priest is Father Ben Beltran of the Smokey Mountain community in Manila. When Fr. Beltran moved to what was the largest garbage slum, he made it his parish and saw every person as a member of that parish. He started by asking everyone, "Who do you think Jesus is?" Through this exercise he discovered that Jesus was already present in the community. This became the thesis of Beltran's doctoral degree and was later

---

[40] Raineer Chu, "Exegeting the City," in *Overture 1: Manila* (Manila, Philippines: Bakke Graduate University, 2014).
[41] Ibid.
[42] Ibid.

published as *The Christology of the Inarticulate: An Inquiry into the Filipino Understanding of Jesus the Christ.*[43]

Beltran said, "No one will follow you unless you spend time with them, it is about relationships".[44] So he spent time with the members of his parish and asked a simple question. As a result, Smokey Mountain is no longer a garbage dump. Through collaborative efforts, Beltran and partners were able to transform the city's garbage collection and processing, launching their own businesses and recycling programs. Veritas Social Empowerment, Inc. runs an IT school and other educational programs, and takes an entrepreneurial approach to working with the poor. The company's slogan, "Imagine. Innovate. Impact." states clearly the vision and intent.[45]

3. From Contextualization to City-wide Movements

The Nestorians knew how to communicate the gospel in the Asian context. Today, the same strategy and skill are needed when talking about the involvement of the international church in urban mission. By definition, the church members and leaders are foreigners and outsiders in the host city. First, I will give a short introduction to the concept of contextualization. Then I will paint a picture of the urban context of Hanoi City, Vietnam's capital. It will become apparent that only through networking and partnerships can the international church be effective. In conclusion, I will introduce several formats of consultations to gather like-minded people for learning from and serving with the city.

The Need for Contextualization

Simply put, "contextualization means doing theology ourselves,"

---

[43] Benigno P. Beltran, *The Christology of the Inarticulate: An Inquiry into the Filipino Understanding of Jesus the Christ* (Manila: Divine Word Publications, 1987).

[44] Benigno Beltran, "Social Empowerment," in *Overture 1: Manila* (Manila, Philippines: Bakke Graduate University, 2014).

[45] Ibid.

explained Dr Tim Gener, President of the Asia Theological Seminary, during our class on Filipino theology in Manila.[46] Doing theology is thinking biblically about something. Thus, Asian contextualization is "thinking biblically in the Asian context". As Gener stated, Christians have "the right to articulate the evangelical traditions in their own terms in light of their own issues".[47]

It was a pleasant surprise to discover a number of theological books in Manila published by the seminaries there. The Asian Theological Seminary (ATS) holds an annual forum and publishes the presenters' papers in book form each year. The publisher, OMF Literature Inc., is working on making these resources available in eBook format. However, the following titles are currently available in print at ATS:

1. *Doing Theology in the Philippines* (2005)

2. *Naming the Unknown God* (2006)

3. *The Church and Poverty in Asia* (2008)

4. *The Earth is the Lord's* (2009)

5. *Walking with God* (2012)[48]

For example, the book *The Church and Poverty in Asia* is a compilation of thirteen papers presented at the fourth Theological Forum in 2008. It represents a broad range of evangelical thought and practice in the Philippines. Based on Mary's song from Luke 1:53, the conference's theme was, "He has filled the hungry with good things". In response, presenters were asked to answer the question, "What is to be our theology of poverty and how are we to

---

[46] Tim Gener, "Filipino Theology," in *Overture 1: Manila* (Manila, Philippines: Bakke Graduate University, 2014).
[47] Ibid.
[48] Asia Theological Forum, "New Books," ed. Jacob Bloemberg (Hanoi: Asia Theological Forum, 2014). Books may be ordered from ATS by sending an email to: theoforum@mail.ats.ph.

make our theology actionable in a fallen world filled with need?"[49] The book is divided in two parts, the first wrestling with the theological and theoretical challenge, and the latter discussing best practices of working among the poor. The forum was hosted at the Union Church of Manila (UCM), the oldest international church in the city.

Another similar book is *Asian Church and God's Mission,* edited by Wonsuk and Julie Ma, former Korean missionaries to the Philippines. This is a collection of papers presented at the *Asian Mission* symposium held in Manila, the Philippines, in 2012. The theme of the conference, "Empowering the Asian Church for God's Mission,"[50] was expounded upon by a selection of sixteen experts in the field. The presenters came from various nations: Honduras, Finland, Burma, Korea, the Philippines, Canada, the USA, Nepal, Japan, and India. The collection is divided into three parts: Reflections, Context, and Strategies. The Asia Pacific Theological Seminary supported the event.

Having lived in Asia for seventeen years, it is the first time that I have come across such rich resources in contextualization. I have collected the books available from ATS and am looking forward to receiving this year's book on the theme, Globalization, Migration, and Diaspora. It is an inspiring idea to think of writing, presenting, collecting, and publishing such papers in my context of Hanoi, Vietnam.

Example: The Urban Context of Hanoi

Hanoi is a unique city. Unlike Manila or Bangkok, it does not have significant slum areas and only few squatter houses. City government has a tight control of the expansion of the city, which is

---

[49] Lee Wanak, ed. *The Church and Poverty in Asia* (Manila, Philippines: OMF Literature Inc., 2008).
[50] Wonsuk Ma and Julie C. Ma, *Asian Church and God's Mission: Studies Presented in the International Symposium on Asian Mission in Manila, January 2002* (Manila, Philippines: OMF Literature, 2003).

a good thing in many ways. Hanoi is also unlike Western cities, which are the focus of so many urban mission textbooks, and unlike African cities, another textbook's favourite context. To start thinking about loving Hanoi, first a clearer picture must be painted of the local context.

When trying to understand who the urban poor are in Hanoi, it is useful to use Viv Grigg's list of eight specialized groups. Segmenting the population helps in creating specialized ministries. Questions to ask are: do these groups have a communal identity, meet one another, have some kind of influence on each other, and is there a church ministry already working among these groups?[51] Below is a listing of these groups with a description of the people for each segment.

1. **Street vendors:** These are the people trying to make a living on and off the streets. Although the city government as restricted street hawkers from the main boulevards and roads, they can be found on many street corners, along sidewalks and in front of shops and homes. From the women selling flowers, bread, kitchen ware, clothes, and pottery off their bicycles to the men and women serving tea and cigarettes, noodle soup, and lunches, or doner kebabs and egg sandwiches, vendors are found everywhere throughout the city. Repairmen ride bicycles through the neighbourhoods calling out for any needed jobs.

2. **Marketplaces:** Long before daybreak, suppliers of produce and meats are riding their motorbikes into the city or deliveries in the multitudes of marketplaces. Mostly run by women, the sellers work from morning to night, living hard lives day in and day out.

3. **Street children:** Because of government efforts to keep children off the streets, these have now gone into hiding. Blue Dragon, an international NGO working to rescue street

_____

[51] Grigg, 46–50.

children, has found one of the hiding places to be on top of a train bridge pillar 25 meters off the ground (see Figure 6). Because sales of postcards or shining shoes are banned, the young boys and girls run a much higher risk of getting involved in the sex trade and being trafficked.[52]

Figure 6: Street Children Living on the Ledge of a Bridge, 80 feet above the Ground[53]

4. **Drug addicts**: With drugs available cheaply, students especially are susceptible to drug addiction. An epidemic problem throughout the city with low success rates at government rehabilitation centres has provided churches in Hanoi with a unique opportunity to be of help. At least five house-based Christian rehab centres are in the city with another ten in surrounding provinces. At least eight to ten churches, including HIF, are collaborating together upon invitation by the government rehab centres to minister there

[52] For more information about the work of Blue Dragon, visit www.bluedragon.org.
[53] Michael Brosowski, "Kids in Danger," Blue Dragon Children's Foundation http://www.bluedragon.org/meet-the-kids/street-kids/kids-in-danger/ (accessed 21 June 2014).

several days per week. Graduates from their three-year program now have the option to join Christian halfway houses in the city.

5. **Alcoholics:** An unrecognized social issue in Vietnamese culture, beer halls and hard drinking are a deeply ingrained problem. Men will spend food money on cheap beer, feeling obliged to drink all hours of the day during business-related meetings, and will drink until they are hospitalized or die of alcohol poisoning. This happened to a friend of mine, who explained that he had to drink in order to win clients for his travel business. Alcoholism is not admitted to be an addiction, but it is everywhere, greatly impacting health, families, and society.

6. **Prostitutes:** Although illegal, prostitutes can be found in most karaoke bars, discos, massage parlours, and hostels. Prostitution is hidden, yet it is always there and available everywhere. Men are almost expected to have extramarital relationships. Prostitutes who are drug addicts will sell their service for as little as $2.50 to get their next dose of heroin. Recently, Christians were given access to a government rehab centre for prostitutes to evangelize among them in hope of transformed lives. When prostitutes leave the centre, government staff tell them to "find a church in the city because they have the answer".[54]

7. **Deaf, blind, and amputees:** Lacking equal opportunities in education and the job market, the handicapped are often kept inside the house or sent to centres. Slow progress is made to integrate them into mainstream society. Several NGOs and social businesses have been successful in providing vocational training and setting up handicraft shops and a bakery café.

8. **Prisoners:** Jail ministry is not yet allowed in Vietnam, except

---

[54] Anonymous source.

for those who minister at the rehab and prostitution centres, which function much like prison camps. It will not be surprising if recovered addicts, prostitutes, and criminals will soon be allowed to start prison ministries because of the testimonies of their transformed lives. It is also unknown to me if there are international prisoners who could possibly be visited by members of our international church. This is a typical ministry provided by fellowships like ours in other nations.

These eight groups can easily be identified in Hanoi. Several others may be added, such as garbage collectors and street sweepers, migrant construction workers, day labourers, students from poor and ethnic families in the provinces, and those with serious health problems awaiting treatment they cannot afford at government hospitals. Clarifying and improving this list with further details and statistics will be most helpful in developing ministries among the urban poor.

The Need for Networks and Partnerships

During my six months of study focused on urban transformation in Manila, the red ribbon running through all the educational experiences is that of partnerships and networking. All the success stories, whether from Veritas or Servant Partners or the Centre for Community Transformation or Grameen Bank, are the results of networking and strategic partnerships between for-profits, non-profits, and government institutions.

Speaking of the success of National Coalition of Urban Transformation (NCUT), founder Corrie DeBoer writes:

> "Networking is the key to the success of this project. Networking helped to reduce the competition in the Christian arena, both among Protestants and between Protestants and Catholics. This study has shown the wisdom and strength of pulling leaders from different churches and religious organizations together to advise each other and seek enlightenment about relations

between organizations and the lessons that can be learned in dialogue. The result has been successfully completed plans because of this pooling of resources and cooperation. Networking has brought about this ecumenical cooperation."[55]

Referencing Marvin Weisbord of Future Search, Corrie explains that for collaborative relationships to succeed, partners must first develop and commit themselves to a set of common goals and objectives. Secondly, they must be willing to contribute their organization's resources to these common goals.[56] DeBoer experienced that, when using the term "collaborate", Catholic and Evangelical seminaries were cautious as it felt too close for them. Instead, the seminaries preferred the term "networking" and organized themselves as a loose alliance under the banner of "Network for Theological Education". As a result, the seminaries "decided to work together in sharing library facilities, faculty, and other resources".[57]

On the other hand, DeBoer experienced "that the urban practitioners were more open to the concept of 'partnership' than the theological educators". She explains:

"Other reasons for interest in partnership were found to be the common ground and interest they held with the other members, the enjoyment of being in partnership in working among the poor, the trust that being in partnership elicited, the ownership to the expected outcomes this partnership provided, and sharing of resources with each other. These characteristics went beyond the descriptions normally ascribed to groups working together."[58]

Looking at the establishment and impact of NCUT as a role model for

---

[55] Lorisa DeBoer, "Developing a Plan for Collaboration in Urban Leadership Development" (Eastern Baptist Theological Seminary, 2000), 90.
[56] Lorisa DeBoer, "Developing a Plan for Collaboration in Urban Leadership Development" (Eastern Baptist Theological Seminary, 2000), 96.
[57] DeBoer, 97.
[58] Ibid.

Love Hanoi, it is clear that we need to gain more understanding of what is meant by networks and partnerships; how these are different from a movement; and how they can be best utilized in our context to serve the goals of Love Hanoi.

Networks and Partnerships Defined

Phil Butler, author of *Well Connected,* believes the brokenness and divisions within the body of Christ to be a great sin. Jesus, right before his betrayal and death, prayed for the unity of the church. "I pray also for those who will believe in me through their message, that all of them may be one, Father, just as you are in me and I am in you. May they also be in us so that the world may believe that you have sent me."[59] It is the Lord's desire for all Christians to be united for the purpose that the world may know that the Father has sent his Son because of his great love for them. Working in collaboration through networking and partnerships is an outward demonstration of God's love.

Butler lists seven primary motivations for and benefits of partnerships and networking: greater efficiency, building on each other's strengths, increased effectiveness, greater flexibility, expanded resources, reduction of risk, and expansion of options for action.[60] Not to confuse networks and partnerships, Butler defines each of them distinctively:

> **Networks:** "Any group of individuals or organizations sharing a common interest, who regularly communicate with each other to enhance *their individual purposes."*

> **Partnerships:** "Any group of individuals or organizations, sharing a common interest, who regularly communicate, plan, and work together *to achieve a common vision beyond the*

---

[59] John 17:20-21 NIV.
[60] Phil Butler, *Well Connected: Releasing the Power and Restoring Hope through Kingdom Partnerships* (Waynesboro, GA: Authentic Media, 2005), 25–26.

capacity of any one of the individual partners."[61]

The key difference between networks and partnerships is the purpose for collaboration, either for their own purposes or for their common goals. "While networks may bring people or organizations together through a common interest," explains Butler, "partnerships galvanize linkages around a common vision or outcome. By working together on that common vision or outcome, they can achieve ends far beyond the capacity of any of the individual members of the partnerships".[62] The book has been made available as a free download at www.connectedbook.net.

From Networks to City-wide Movements

In his book, *The Good City*, Glenn Barth outlines the six "stages of development for organizations serving city movements". [63] These six stages are as follows: exploration, formation, operation, breakthrough, transformation, and replication.[64] Each stage requires different functions and skills by the movement leader. The table below shows how movements develop and what kind of leadership is needed from stage to stage.

In 2012, inspired by Swanson and William's book, *To Transform a City*,[65] HIF launched the "Love Hanoi" campaign. To get the movement off the ground, we first had to go through the exploration stage. Barth states, "Exploration is a foundational stage and must be given adequate time for relational equity to develop".[66] For stage one, the leader needs to be a catalyst and visionary with the skill set of being relational, a good communicator, and able to convene mixed

---

[61] Phil Butler, *Well Connected: Releasing the Power and Restoring Hope through Kingdom Partnerships* (Waynesboro, GA: Authentic Media, 2005), 34–35.
[62] Butler, 35.
[63] Glenn Barth, *The Good City* (Tallmadge, OH: S.D. Myers Publishing Services, 2010), 41.
[64] Ibid.
[65] Swanson and Williams.
[66] Barth, 43.

groups of people.

Table 3: Stages of Development[67]

Stage	Function	Skill
Exploration	Catalyst Visionary	Relational Communication Convening
Formation	Visionary	Communication Facilitating Management Creative Thinking
Operation	Management	Decision Making People Building Motivational
Breakthrough	Prayer	Doing the right things at the right times
Transformation	Discipling	Presence-based Prayer
Replication	Teaching	Training and Coaching Skills

Referencing Butler's Process of Partnership Exploration from *Well Connected*, Barth lists six parts to stage one: gathering initial information; doing initial interviews; reviewing and expanding information; doing further interviews; drawing initial conclusions; and deciding whether or not to move to the formation stage.[68] Currently, I am the champion of the Love Hanoi movement, which at some point will need to transfer to another leader.

Now, Love Hanoi needs to transition to the next phase. "Formation is a critical stage that can only be entered into when there is evidence of significant buy-in from, and relational equity built, with key leaders around the vision for the development of a coalition to lead a city movement," writes Barth.[69] Formation is needed for the organization of the movement to go operational. It is critical that Love Hanoi passes through this stage in the coming year to avoid either getting stuck in exploration indefinitely or remaining solely an

---

[67] Barth.
[68] Ibid.
[69] Barth, 47.

HIF campaign. Often I am asked, what is Love Hanoi? It is therefore helpful to clarify the differences between a campaign, movement, network, and partnership and how they all relate.

Campaign: As the initiator of Love Hanoi, HIF is the owner of what would be best defined as a campaign to promote loving the city. It is not a program or project (although in Vietnamese the word "dự án" is broader in meaning). It is more like an idea or initiative. It is not a committee and does not have a structure or budget, which would likely kill it. It is a promotional campaign in the way the word is used in advertising, to promote the idea of loving the city. In translation to Vietnamese, it is important to use appropriate language to avoid making it sound like a military campaign or like the Christian crusades of the middle ages.

Movement: The vision is for Love Hanoi to become a movement, to inspire collaboration among churches and across the three sectors of society (public, profit, and non-profit). Love Hanoi will likely not become an organization, but remain as a vision and inspirational idea. A good example is the "I'm a City Changer" campaign, which is described as "a global movement to share and spread individual, corporate, and public initiatives that improve our cities". As the website states, "I'm a City Changer campaign is convened by UN-Habitat, the United Nations Human Settlements Programme, with support from partners from the private and public sector".[70] This vocabulary is very helpful and has been adapted to describe the Love Hanoi campaign in our brochure and website as follows: "Love Hanoi is a campaign to inspire and mobilize individual, corporate, and public initiatives for the benefit of the city. It is promoted by City Partnerships, the charity arm of Hanoi International Fellowship".[71] This wording works well in our expatriate context.

On the other hand, Love Hanoi could become organized and have various working groups and discussion forums working on specific

---

[70] UN-Habitat, "I'm a City Changer", UN-Habitat http://imacitychanger.org/ (accessed 19 June 2014).
[71] For more information, visit www.lovehanoi.org.

issues. Taking the Lausanne Movement as an example, it defines itself as "a global movement that mobilizes evangelical leaders to collaborate for world evangelization. Together we seek to bear witness to Jesus Christ and all his teaching, in every part of the world — not only geographically, but in every sphere of society and in the realm of ideas". Lausanne's purpose statement is, "Calling the Whole Church to take the Whole Gospel to the Whole World". [72] If Love Hanoi were to become solely an evangelical movement, the Lausanne statement could be adapted as Bakke and Swanson use it: Calling the Whole Church to take the Whole Gospel to the Whole City. This, however, may be too evangelistic for our expatriate and political contexts, hindering us in building relationships with government and non-Christian organizations. At this time, it would be better to use the language from UN-Habitat and integrate it with biblical references and perspectives such as Jeremiah 29:7, to "seek the peace and prosperity of the city" and to "pray for it".

Networks: Although Love Hanoi is already creating an informal network through relationship building, consultations, and joint projects, the question is, should Love Hanoi organize itself as a network. As a movement, Love Hanoi can give birth to networks, such as a network for non-profit organizations, an association of Christian drug rehabs, or a coalition for promoting integration of the handicapped in mainstream education. If Love Hanoi were to become a network, it may limit the freedom to start other networks.

Yet, the need for a network is there and was clearly identified during our informal workgroup meeting. Like NCUT in the Philippines, a network is needed to unite and strengthen the various efforts for urban transformation. NCUT became the mother of other networks, groups, and organizations. The idea of a national coalition also increases the scope from focusing on one city to expanding nationwide, learning from and strengthening urban transformation initiatives throughout Vietnam. This might be a good reason not to

---

[72] The Lausanne Movement, "Faqs", The Lausanne Movement http://www.lausanne.org/en/about/faqs.html (accessed 19 June 2014).

call it the Love Hanoi Network, but perhaps the Hanoi Network for Urban Transformation and later change it to a national network.

Partnerships: It is only through relationships that God's love can be expressed more fully and completely. Love Hanoi as a movement can become an incubator for networks and partnerships. As DeBoer learned in Manila, some organizations and individuals may be more comfortable staying at the network level, while others are more eager to collaborate closely on shared projects. Partnerships not only strengthen each partner and provide synergy to accomplish the goal, they also are a witness of the unity among Christians to outsiders. During the previous Tet Holiday visit by ECVN, HIF, and a Korean Baptist church with the National Religious Affairs office, the Vice Director encouraged increased partnerships among the churches, specifically to do social work. The Easter concert was a display of partnership and collaboration, praised by city government. These partnerships can now be extended into other realms of ministry to express God's love for the city.

City Consultations: Big and Small

In order to connect more people, build networks, and create partnerships, the Love Hanoi Movement can implement more and varied consultations. Bakke and Sharpe give a number of ideas for one-day consultations and provide an outline for a three-day, city-wide consultation. Examples of one-day models are as follows:[73]

- City Ministry Summit: celebrate signs of hope, address most pressing issues

- New Pastors Orientation: introduce to civic leaders, ministries, congregations

- City Tour: expose church members, leaders, pastors to the city

---

[73] The models listed and quotations are quoted from Raymond J. Bakke and Jon Sharpe, *Street Signs : A New Direction in Urban Ministry* (Birmingham, Ala.: New Hope Publishers, 2006), 246-256.

- Think Tank: one issue, sharing, present papers, action steps

- Denominational Consultation: assess urban ministry nationally and internationally

- Academic Seminars: one week, lectures and immersion, academic credit

- Three-day consultation: city-wide catalyst for creating partnerships and initiatives

A possible course of action for the Love Hanoi Movement to move forward is to establish what Bakke and Sharpe call the Envisioning Team which will organize on-going consultations, leading up to a three-day, city-wide event. Sharpe explains,

"A team capable of networking widely in the city and providing the necessary resources to do good research is vital. This team should represent diverse ministries, churches, mission organizations, educational institutions, and ethnic groups and should have whole church connections. The team should include Roman Catholic, orthodox, mainline, evangelical, and Pentecostal representatives, as well as people from ministries working with homelessness, poverty, refugees, youth at risk, and other social issues."[74]

To find such team members, we need to ask the question, "Who knows everybody, and who can we trust?"[75] For example, Corrie DeBoer is mentioned as being the person in Manila with relational capital. Who are the Vietnamese and expatriate "Corries" in Hanoi? Who is a networker, has the influence to gather people across denominational and organizational lines, and has the relational capital needed to make this team successful? From what denominations and organizations do we want to pick these

---

[74] Raymond J. Bakke and Jon Sharpe, *Street Signs: A New Direction in Urban Ministry* (Birmingham, Ala.: New Hope Publishers, 2006), 220.
[75] Bakke and Sharpe, 221.

members? In addition to networkers, the team will need people with analytical skills and experience in the socio-economic and political realm as well as people with administrative skills.

Conclusion

The book of Acts tells the story of the first-century, missional, international church movement. Originating in Antioch of Syria, this movement spread not only westwards, but also to the Eastern and Southern hemispheres. The church thrived in urban centres, some known for their many chapels and cathedrals. The diaspora of the early centuries made it possible for the gospel to spread through word and deed.

Today, the global diaspora is at a high point with almost one billion displaced around the world. Almost a quarter of those are intentionally and predominantly moving from rural to urban areas, from East to West, and from South to North. These are expatriates who, if they are Christian, find themselves attending international churches. The Global Diaspora Network and the Missional International Church Network see this as an opportunity to minister to, through, and beyond the diaspora. International churches are uniquely positioned to make an impact.

To do so, a number of things must be taken into consideration: What is the role of the international church and of the affluent church? What is the role of the pastor of such churches? Viv Grigg has helped to understand these roles and Catholic priests have shown us how to make the city our parish.

Finally, I have outlined how international churches can move within their given context to become missionally engaged through partnerships, networking, and starting a city-wide movement to love their cities. Using HIF and the Love Hanoi movement as an example, I have illustrated how international churches can be effective in urban mission around the globe. If it is possible in Hanoi, it surely can be done elsewhere.

Appendix: Three-Day Urban Consultation Agenda[76]

Concept: Bring together key people in the city to discover the signs of hope in the city, in a sense to cooperate with the Lord in the city. The consultation is designed to bring people together, through a broad spectrum, to get a greater grasp.

"Whole church, whole gospel to transform the whole city."

Anticipates: 100–200 people in attendance

FIRST DAY

Evening: 7:00 pm – 9:45 pm

- Start off with case studies/ video (1 hour)

- Singing (30 minutes)

- Divide people in small groups (15 minutes)

    o What did they come looking for? (30 minutes)

    o What do they want to go home with?

- Write responses on post-it board paper and maybe have three or four teams share (30 minutes). Their answers to these questions will serve as a "contract" for them.

SECOND DAY

Morning: 9:00 am – 12:30 pm

Refreshments

- Signs of hope for the city (60 to 90 minutes: 6 individuals, 10–15 minutes each); Government leaders, non-profit leaders, business leaders: maybe three leaders share with everyone.

---

[76] Bakke and Sharpe, 279–280.

- Divide into small groups:

  o Share the signs of hope for the city

  o Needs: what are the needs for the city

- Lunch.

Afternoon: 2:30 pm – 5:30 pm

- Visit sites: See ministry in action — homeless, orphans, street kids, government people, education, tutoring. Have about fifteen available sites, each group will visit approximately three (duration: about five hours). Notice powerful vs. powerless.

- Social event?

THIRD DAY

- Visit a few more sites

- Talk about what we have seen, what we have heard

- Ray Bakke speaks

- In groups: what should be done about it? New network/new relationships.

References

Asia Theological Forum. "New Books." edited by Jacob Bloemberg. Hanoi: Asia Theological Forum, 2014.

Bakke, Lowell. "Introduction." In *Overture 1: Manila*. Manila, Philippines: Bakke Graduate University, 2014.

Bakke, Raymond J. and Jon Sharpe. *Street Signs : A New Direction in Urban Ministry*. Birmingham, Ala.: New Hope Publishers, 2006.

Barth, Glenn. *The Good City*. Tallmadge, OH: S.D. Myers Publishing Services, 2010.

Beltran, Benigno. "Social Empowerment." In *Overture 1: Manila*. Manila, Philippines: Bakke Graduate University, 2014.

Beltran, Benigno P. *The Christology of the Inarticulate : An Inquiry into the Filipino Understanding of Jesus the Christ*. Manila: Divine Word Publications, 1987.

Brosowski, Michael, "Kids in Danger", Blue Dragon Children's Foundation http://www.bluedragon.org/meet-the-kids/street-kids/kids-in-danger/ (accessed 21 June 2014).

Butler, Phil. *Well Connected: Releasing the Power and Restoring Hope through Kingdom Partnerships*. Waynesboro, GA: Authentic Media, 2005.

Chu, Raineer. "Exegeting the City." In *Overture 1: Manila*. Manila, Philippines: Bakke Graduate University, 2014.

DeBoer, Lorisa. "Developing a Plan for Collaboration in Urban Leadership Development." Eastern Baptist Theological Seminary, 2000.

Gener, Tim. "Filippino Theology." In *Overture 1: Manila*. Manila, Philippines: Bakke Graduate University, 2014.

Grigg, Viv. *Cry of the Urban Poor*. Monrovia, Calif.: MARC, 1992.

Jenkins, Philip. *The Lost History of Christianity : The Thousand-Year Golden Age of the Church in the Middle East, Africa, and Asia- and How It Died*. 1st ed. New York: HarperOne, 2008.

Ma, Wonsuk and Julie C. Ma. *Asian Church and God's Mission : Studies Presented in the International Symposium on Asian Mission in Manila, January 2002*. Manila, Philippines: OMF Literature, 2003.

Sander, Nikola, Guy Abel and Ramon Bauer, "The Global Flow of People", Wittgenstein Centre for Demography and Global Human Capital http://www.global-migration.info/ (accessed 29 March 2014).

Swanson, Eric and Sam Williams. *To Transform a City: Whole Church, Whole Gospel, Whole City*. Grand Rapids, MI: Zondervan, 2010.

The Lausanne Movement, "Faqs", The Lausanne Movement http://www.lausanne.org/en/about/faqs.html (accessed 19 June 2014).

Tira, Sadiri Joy, ed. *The Human Tidal Wave*. Pasig City, Philippines: Lifechange Publishing, Inc., 2013.

UN-Habitat, "I'm a City Changer", UN-Habitat http://imacitychanger.org/ (accessed 19 June 2014).

USF Ricci Institute, "The Lotus and the Cross: East-West Cultural Exchange Along the Silk Road ", University of San Fransisco (accessed 4 June 2014).

Wanak, Lee, ed. *The Church and Poverty in Asia*. Manila, Philippines: OMF Literature Inc., 2008.

CHAPTER EIGHT
MULTICULTURAL CHURCHES IN GLOBAL CITIES

By Michael Crane, ThM, PhD
Director / Consultant Radius Initiatives
Professor of Urban Missiology
Malaysian Baptist Theological Seminary
Pulau Pinang, Malaysia

Michael D. Crane (Ph.D.) along with his wife and two sons, lives in Southeast Asia teaching at two seminaries and training urban church planters. Michael is passionate about equipping Christians to engage the growing cities around the world. He was raised overseas and was discipled at an international church in Manila during high school. Michael has written a number of articles and a book titled Sowing Seeds of Change: Cultivating Transformation in the City (forthcoming).

Many of the great missionaries of Christian history have been those who knew their world as well as anyone. Paul, for example seemed very familiar with the most influential centers of the Roman Empire.[77] William Carey compiled an impressive collection of global

---

[77] Paul's awareness of geography and politics allowed him to continue his missionary work when impeded on a few occasions. Eckhard J. Schnabel, *Paul*

statistics two hundred years before the internet.[78] The call of the Great Commission to make disciples of every nation, means we must know our world. To add to this challenge, the world of our day is rapidly changing due to the twin forces of globalization and urbanization. In order to effectively make disciples of every nation, we need to understand our world and adapt our ministries, maximizing our ability to be ministers of the gospel.

The Nations are on the Move...to Cities All Over the World

Every hour thousands of people pick up their lives and move to a city. Global population growth in this century will primarily take place in cities. Ray Bakke calls it the greatest migration in history.[79] Viv Grigg calls this the urban millennium.[80] This rapid movement of humanity to the cities might be the most memorable fact of our century.[81] Urbanization is not only about sheer numbers of people moving to cities; it is changing people, cultures, and societies at large.

Cities punch above their weight in terms of global impact. Influence and innovation ripple out from cities to the rest of the world. They have managed to accumulate high caliber leaders, thinkers, and creators from all over the world. And, because media is primarily urban, news of new products and policies spreads far beyond metropolitan areas. In other words, the average urban dweller has more influence on the world than someone in a rural setting.

---

the *Missionary: Realities, Strategies and Methods* (Downers Grove, IL: IVP Academic, 2008), 223.

[78] Timothy C. Tennent, "William Carey as a Missiologist: An Assessment," in *Expect Great Things, Attempt Great Things: William Carey and Adoniram Judson, Missionary Pioneers*, ed. Allen Yeh and Chris Chun (Eugene, OR: Wipf & Stock Publishers, 2013), 25.

[79] Raymond Bakke and Jon Sharpe, *Street Signs : A New Direction in Urban Ministry* (Birmingham, AL: New Hope Publishers, 2006), 81.

[80] Viv Grigg, *The Spirit of Christ and the Postmodern City: Transforming Revival Among Auckland's Evangelicals and Pentecostals* (Lexington, KY: Emeth Press, 2009), 26.

[81] Doug Saunders, *Arrival City: How the Largest Migration in History Is Reshaping Our World* (New York: Pantheon Books, 2010), 1.

People and cultures change when they become urbanized. When someone moves from a village in India to Mumbai, a city of more than 18 million people, he or she goes through irrevocable changes. Everything is different, from social interactions to work patterns to modes of survival. The diversity and density of cities uploads a range ideas and emotions that exceeds the norms for a village dweller. More often than not, this village dweller who moves to the city will never be the same.

Increasingly, people are not merely moving to the large city nearby, they are crossing international borders looking for employment, education, or escape. This shift is even more dramatic because there is less in this large, multicultural city that is familiar. I had a seminary student who arrived from a small, rural village in Myanmar. Everything seemed overwhelming, you could see it in his eyes. He was uncomfortable with technology and elevators made him uneasy. A year down the road, he was an entirely different person. He was casually communicating on his smart phone, getting around on a subway, working in the midst of the commercial district surrounded by four star hotels and world class shopping malls. As thousands are added to our cities every hour, the amount of cultural change is almost beyond comprehension.

Although people who have been urbanized have gone through tremendous changes, churches have not. My Burmese student is expected to minister in exactly the same way he would if he was still in that small rural village. Every day he interacts with urban professionals from all over the world who are working in this global city. The church has not adapted to the realities of a rapidly urbanizing world. Patrick Johnstone alerts us to this reality: "Too many of us are hankering or preparing for a world that no longer exists."[82] We need churches that are able to minister to urbanized people.

---

[82] Patrick Johnstone, *The Future of the Global Church: History, Trends and Possibilities* (Downers Grove, IL: IVP Books, 2011), 6.

Hollywood, Bollywood, and Nollywood : Globalized Daily Living

During my travels around the world when I tell people that I am from California, more often than not, they will say something about Hollywood. Such is the vast influence of the American movie industry. Hollywood's popularity means far more than an economic boom for Southern California; these movies spread ideas, ways of life, and even culture. However, it might surprise us to know that the United States only ranks third among nations producing the most movies. India produces more movies than any other country in the world. Their movie industry, often called Bollywood[83] (which, strictly speaking, is only a portion of the Indian movie industry), has become popular all over the world. These dramatic films infused with song and dance have gained a faithful following on every continent. Nigeria boasts the second largest movie industry in the world. Dubbed Nollywood, Nigeria's movie industry brings in over 10 billion dollars a year and is popular throughout the African continent and gaining popularity around the world. Digital filming technology and distribution through the internet makes global viewership a reality.

At one time, culture was more easily confined to geography. These thriving movie industries along with television and music industries (i.e. telenovelas out of Latin America and K-pop out of South Korea) are exporting more than entertainment. They are spreading cultural ideas and trends. The notion of the tribal native who knows only his own music and culture is becoming rare. Around the world, people are becoming culturally globalized. Moreover, the spread of entertainment is no longer only from the West, but it now goes in every direction.

Education has become a globalized industry. More and more young people are going across borders to study in universities. The trend used to be students going to a few English-speaking Western

---

[83] Bollywood is a portmanteau combining Bombay (the former name of modern day Mumbai, India) with Hollywood. Much of the Hindi language movie production comes from the industry in Mumbai.

countries for university education. This is no longer the case. Millions of students are going all over the world to study. Not only are students going global, but universities are, as well. For example, the University of Nottingham has moved beyond one campus in England. They now have full campuses in Ningbo, China and Semenyih, Malaysia, attracting students from every corner of the globe. The reason for the university's global stretch is posted on their website: "Internationalisation is at the heart of everything we do as a university."[84] I have come to know a number of graduates of this university and have seen them take jobs in cities all over the world working for multinational corporations like BP, Intel, Bechtal, and Accenture. They are the new citizens of a global, urban professional class. Even those who return to their home country often find that they are more comfortable among the international community. Internationalized universities are creating culturally globalized citizens who are seeking to be a part of a like-minded community.

In addition to the millions who cross borders to study, there are 215 million international migrants.[85] Statistics are difficult to track because there is so much fluctuation of peoples travelling to other lands for work or to escape troubled circumstances. In my neighborhood in a Southeast Asian city I can stroll from my home to my office and easily encounter people from Nepal, Kazakhstan, Pakistan, China, France, Nigeria, Russia, and Mongolia. The presence of such an international community even changes those who have not crossed borders. Cultures around the world remain distinctive in many ways but they are also becoming globalized. An Economist article a few years ago noted that, for the first time in history, it is normal to be foreign.[86] Cities like London and New York have been intersections of the nations for decades. Now cities like Guangzhou

---

[84] "The University of Nottingham," February 9, 2015, http://www.nottingham.ac.uk/.

[85] Phillip Connor, *Immigrant Faith: Patterns of Immigrant Religion in the United States, Canada, and Western Europe* (New York: NYU Press, 2014), 16.

[86] "Being Foreign: The Others," *The Economist*, December 17, 2009, http://www.economist.com/node/15108690.

in China have a section of the city devoted to selling goods to Africans living in the city.[87] Cities are rapidly becoming more multicultural.

People are moving all over the world for one reason or another. Patrick Johnstone urges the church to reflect on the implications of globalization for ministry:

The scale of movement of people from one continent to another is unprecedented in history, and will be a major preoccupation for governments for much of the 21st Century. It is vital that we all realize the social, cultural, economic, political and spiritual implications and prepare for this inevitable, unstoppable reality.[88]

The forces of globalization and urbanization have fostered an increased multiculturalism that is changing societies, particularly the urban ones. Even as so much change has occurred, the church lags behind. It is time to plant churches in cities all over the world that cater to this growing segment of the world's population.

Global Trends Creating the Need for International Churches

We have seen the big picture impact of urbanization and globalization. In the midst of these world-changing movements there are a few trends that create an open door for multicultural churches in international cities.

English is the New Latin

As the world globalizes, the number of languages spoken around the world is in steady decline. It is economically advantageous to master a global language. More people from more diverse parts of the world are speaking fewer languages.[89] English is a leader among global

---

[87] "Africans in Guangzhou," *People's Daily Online- English*, April 24, 2014, http://en.people.cn/98649/8607801.html.
[88] Johnstone, *The Future of the Global Church*, 4.
[89] Harm De Blij, *The Power of Place: Geography, Destiny, and Globalization's Rough Landscape* (Oxford; New York: Oxford University Press, 2009), 32–34,

languages and is the most important language in international business.[90]

At one time English was the language of the West brought with colonization. This is no longer the case. All around the world English is used in parliamentary meetings, business negotiations and university lectures. For many millions English is a first language, and for billions more it is an important second language. The second largest English speaking population in the world is in India, and it is the only language spoken in every part of the country.[91] Even in countries that do not use English heavily, like Indonesia, English is still a required subject in every year of grade school, and universities often use English textbooks for most science and math courses. Those working in multi-national corporations or institutions must be conversant in English. After the tsunami struck the shores of Indonesia over ten years ago, more than 800 disaster relief organizations from all over the world provided assistance. English was the language of inter-agency meetings and in most offices.

When I think of my Kazakh neighbor in Southeast Asia, there is little chance of finding a Kazakh church or even one worshipping in Russian. His primary opportunity to hear the gospel is through an English-speaking multicultural church. While the loss of so many languages is lamentable, it provides an opportunity for multicultural churches to be planted.

A Palette of Choices

When people move to another country they are uprooted from their normal cultural constructs. Global cities cater to the vast diversity of

---

http://www.barnesandnoble.com/w/the-power-of-place-harm-de-blij/1116790708.

[90] Dorie Clark, "English - The Language of Global Business?," *Forbes*, October 26, 2012, http://www.forbes.com/sites/dorieclark/2012/10/26/english-the-language-of-global-business/.

[91] Brian Stanley, *The Global Diffusion of Evangelicalism: The Age of Billy Graham and John Stott*, vol. Vol. 5, A History of Evangelicalism (Downers Grove, IL: IVP Academic, 2013), 22.

the world in terms of entertainment as well as worship. For those who are already Christians, there is a need for an international community of Christians who can welcome them. Without this option, well-intentioned Christians can become unmoored from their faith foundation. For those who are not Christians, the presence of a multicultural church offers the perfect opportunity to "try out" Christianity.

The diversity of cities means an urbanite has a palette of options. Urbanites have grown accustomed to options, whether it is a choice of doctors, stockbrokers, or baristas. This is as true religiously as it is culturally. Rodney Stark studied the spread of Christianity in the early church in *Cities of God*. He not only sees Christianity as an urban movement, but he notes that churches were established first in those cities that were most heterogeneous (diverse).[92] From these cities Christianity took root among the diverse citizens and spread to other cities and the countryside. The presence of people from other cultures and temples of other faiths increased the likelihood of Christianity becoming established there.[93]

Today, global cities can serve the same function as those Roman cities located on trade routes in the 1st and 2nd centuries. Establishing multicultural churches in global cities, even in countries with minimal Christian presence, can become a launching point for more churches to be planted in the region.

New Points of Contact

My friend Andrew[94] was raised in Bucharest, Romania. His early life was influenced by communist atheism. As communism decreased, Andrew saw the importance of global financial services and knew he needed to master English. There was an international church in his

---

[92] Rodney Stark, *Cities of God: The Real Story of How Christianity Became an Urban Movement and Conquered Rome* (San Francisco: HarperSanFrancisco, 2006), 79–81.
[93] Ibid., 80, 113.
[94] Andrew's name is changed out of respect for his privacy.

city that offered English classes. Andrew went to the English church services for further English practice. He came to faith in Christ through the teaching at the international church and now lives in a predominantly Muslim city working in the banking industry as a witness of the gospel.

By the time Andrew began to attend the international churches there were plenty of local, Romanian churches he could have attended. But for Andrew his initial interest was not in Christianity, but in English. International churches are not merely for expatriates in a foreign land, but can draw many locals who, for one reason or another, would not have attended local churches. Some are attracted to the multicultural nature of the church, others are drawn to those who work in similar careers, and others may see an international church as a better fit culturally than local churches. In any case, international churches can be an initial point of contact for someone who has never heard the gospel.

A Great Commission-Sized Opportunity

The church has a primary calling to be a multiplicative witness to Christ in the world (Acts 1:8). The substance of that calling is to make disciples who know Christ and follow the teachings of Christ of every nation (Matt. 28:18-20). We must now proceed to make the connection between these trends of urbanization and globalization and the calling of the church to be Christ's witnesses.

Making Disciples of All Nations

Our calling is to make disciples of all nations. Remarkably, God has brought the nations to our cities. "Those most likely to be the least evangelized at the end of the twentieth century have congregated in the urban centers of the world."[95] In many rural areas it is common to find only the elderly and children. The young adults have all gone to the cities. There are over 300 hundred different languages spoken

---

[95] Judy Raymo, "Urban Pilgrims and Pioneers: WEC International and the World's Cities," *Urban Mission*, June 1998, 43.

in London.[96] Countries like India are made up of hundreds of different linguistic groups. The city of Chennai alone has 200 migrant groups.[97] The nations have come to the cities and are more open to the gospel than in their home towns. I have seen friends baptized who come from extremely oppressive environments. Their entry into a large, multicultural city allows them the space to explore Christianity without fear of imprisonment or death. Due to the more public profile of a multicultural church, there are many opportunities to lead to faith those who have never heard the gospel.

People groups appear to be more culturally distinct in their rural settings. Traditional missions strategies have focused on starting churches that appeal to these traditional cultures. When people move into cities, they become more culturally blended. Many intermarry with those from other people groups. Traditional cultural identity fades for many urbanites as they become global citizens. Our missions strategies need to catch up to these contemporary realities. As the nations move to cities, they become intermingled and complex. Multicultural churches are needed to disciple all the nations arriving in the cities.

Discipleship at Critical Times

Another friend got a lucrative job in a global city as an engineer. He and his family were Christians and visited several local, English-speaking churches in their city. Each visit was more discouraging than the one before. They felt culturally at odds with the more homogeneous culture of the local churches. Soon they gave up trying to attend a church. Each month away from any Christian community created doubts about their faith and their children were growing up without any connection to the church. When an international church was started in their neighborhood, they decided to give church one more try. Immediately, they felt at home amongst this multicultural

---

[96] Phil Wood and Charles Landry, *The Intercultural City: Planning for Diversity Advantage* (London; Sterling, VA: Routledge, 2007), 25.
[97] Samuel Saravanan, "Urban Evangelism in India: A Missiological Exploration," *Hindustan Evangelical Review* 7 (2014 2013): 26.

blend of people. Soon the whole family was connected into the church, their children were baptized, and they were all growing as disciples.

Moving to another country can be enormously disrupting to a person. At such critical points of transition it is easy to lose a firm grip on one's core beliefs. Multicultural churches provide an important service in helping people grow in their faith in Christ in the midst of personal turbulence. Whether the person is suddenly working in a lucrative job with all of the expatriate compensation benefits or a migrant worker living off a meagre wage, moving to another country opens the door for temptations and life complications never before faced. Couples may go overseas happily married and return to their home country divorced. A vibrant multicultural church community can be ready to provide biblical counsel and community.

The church also has an opportunity to reach out to people with the life-giving good news of Jesus Christ during these times of transition. Studies have shown people have a higher receptivity to the gospel upon arriving in a new city.[98] There are some who move from city to city every few years. The only opportunity for some so transient to hear the gospel is through the outreach of a multicultural church.

Multicultural Churches: A Signpost of the Gospel

In two places in Revelation (5:9 and 7:9) we are given beautiful snapshots of worship in the life to come. In both passages the worship includes people from every nation, tribe, people, and language. It is the ultimate fulfillment of God's promise to Abraham in Genesis 12:1-3, that all the nations would be blessed through him. It also provides hope as we are sent out to make disciples of all

---

[98] David Hesselgrave, *Planting Churches Cross-Culturally: A Guide for Home and Foreign Missions* (Grand Rapids Mich.: Baker Book House, 1980), 99; Paul Hiebert and Eloise Meneses, *Incarnational Ministry: Planting Churches in Band, Tribal, Peasant, and Urban Societies* (Grand Rapids: Baker Books, 1995), 273.

nations (Matt. 28:18-20). Our destiny, as believers in Christ, is supremely multicultural.

The current divisions and discord between different ethnic groups is not a sign of hope but rather of brokenness. Jesus entered a world torn by division and discord. In his death and resurrection he has eviscerated the "dividing wall of hostility" (Eph. 2:14, ESV). Through his blood all things have been reconciled (Col. 1:20). In other words, Christ's work on the cross was not merely for the sake of individuals; he was drawing us together as one new humanity.[99] For the early church this was not mere theory. We can see from the church in Antioch and through the letters that Paul wrote to churches that the church was intended to display God's new humanity. The coming together of ethnic groups as one body is directly reflective of the work of Christ. Multicultural churches today can stand as remarkable displays of the gospel.

Cities are the quintessential gathering points of humanity. The church has an incredible opportunity to display Christ's marvelous work of reconciliation as they work to start and lead multicultural churches. Troy Bush, pastoring in a multicultural area of Atlanta, says: "Each congregation in the city should be moving toward the inclusion of all peoples that seek after God and become followers of Jesus Christ..."[100] Multicultural churches play a vital role in fulfilling the Great Commission.

Conclusion

A deeper understanding of our world and our calling should inform the ways we minister in our world. Urbanization is drawing people to our growing cities. Globalization is creating a mix of cultures and peoples in our cities. Just as Paul was able to use the common language of Greek to start churches throughout the Roman Empire,

---

[99] David E. Stevens, *God's New Humanity: A Biblical Theology of Multiethnicity for the Church* (Eugene, OR: Wipf & Stock Publishers, 2012), 96.
[100] Troy L. Bush, "Urbanizing Panta Ta Ethnē," *Journal of Evangelism and Missions* 12 (n.d.): 13.

we have an opportunity to use the common language of English to start churches in cities throughout the world. With the incredible blending of cultures and peoples in our cities, multicultural churches are able to be vital partners in fulfilling the Great Commission. International churches are uniquely positioned to display the work of Christ in making us one new humanity.

Works Cited

"Africans in Guangzhou." *People's Daily Online- English*, April 24, 2014. http://en.people.cn/98649/8607801.html.

Bakke, Raymond, and Jon Sharpe. *Street Signs : A New Direction in Urban Ministry*. Birmingham, AL: New Hope Publishers, 2006.

"Being Foreign: The Others." *The Economist*, December 17, 2009. http://www.economist.com/node/15108690.

Bush, Troy L. "Urbanizing Panta Ta Ethnē." *Journal of Evangelism and Missions* 12 (n.d.).

Clark, Dorie. "English - The Language of Global Business?" *Forbes*, October 26, 2012. http://www.forbes.com/sites/dorieclark/2012/10/26/english-the-language-of-global-business/.

Connor, Phillip. *Immigrant Faith: Patterns of Immigrant Religion in the United States, Canada, and Western Europe*. New York: NYU Press, 2014.

De Blij, Harm. *The Power of Place: Geography, Destiny, and Globalization's Rough Landscape*. Oxford; New York: Oxford University Press, 2009. http://www.barnesandnoble.com/w/the-power-of-place-harm-de-blij/1116790708.

Grigg, Viv. *The Spirit of Christ and the Postmodern City: Transforming Revival Among Auckland's Evangelicals and Pentecostals*. Lexington, KY: Emeth Press, 2009.

Hesselgrave, David. *Planting Churches Cross-Culturally: A Guide for Home and Foreign Missions*. Grand Rapids Mich.: Baker Book House, 1980.

Hiebert, Paul, and Eloise Meneses. *Incarnational Ministry: Planting Churches in Band, Tribal, Peasant, and Urban Societies*. Grand Rapids:

Baker Books, 1995.

Johnstone, Patrick. *The Future of the Global Church: History, Trends and Possibilities*. Downers Grove, IL: IVP Books, 2011.

Raymo, Judy. "Urban Pilgrims and Pioneers: WEC International and the World's Cities." *Urban Mission*, June 1998, 43–47.

Saravanan, Samuel. "Urban Evangelism in India: A Missiological Exploration." *Hindustan Evangelical Review* 7 (2014 2013): 25–49.

Saunders, Doug. *Arrival City: How the Largest Migration in History Is Reshaping Our World*. New York: Pantheon Books, 2010.

Schnabel, Eckhard J. *Paul the Missionary: Realities, Strategies and Methods*. Downers Grove, IL: IVP Academic, 2008.

Stanley, Brian. *The Global Diffusion of Evangelicalism: The Age of Billy Graham and John Stott*. Vol. Vol. 5. A History of Evangelicalism. Downers Grove, IL: IVP Academic, 2013.

Stark, Rodney. *Cities of God: The Real Story of How Christianity Became an Urban Movement and Conquered Rome*. San Francisco: HarperSanFrancisco, 2006.

Stevens, David E. *God's New Humanity: A Biblical Theology of Multiethnicity for the Church*. Eugene, OR: Wipf & Stock Publishers, 2012.

Tennent, Timothy C. "William Carey as a Missiologist: An Assessment." In *Expect Great Things, Attempt Great Things: William Carey and Adoniram Judson, Missionary Pioneers*, edited by Allen Yeh and Chris Chun, 15–26. Eugene, OR: Wipf & Stock Publishers, 2013.

"The University of Nottingham," February 9, 2015. http://www.nottingham.ac.uk/.

Wood, Phil, and Charles Landry. *The Intercultural City: Planning for Diversity Advantage*. London; Sterling, VA: Routledge, 2007.

CHAPTER NINE
RESPONSES OF INTERNATIONAL CHURCH PASTORS TO TEN SURVEY QUESTIONS

We surveyed several pastors of international or military churches, and received the following answers. It is clear from the responses that some multicultural exposure helped to prepare the pastors for their assignment, that turnover is one of the greatest challenges they face, that being open and listening to people was important for effective ministry, and that many of the basic tools to build and grow churches in one setting translates into others.

The pastors whose responses are given below are:

- Erik Nielsen, Pastor of First International Baptist Church, Copennagen, Denmark
- Scott Chadwick, Pastor of International Baptist Church, Sofia, Bulgaria
- James Goforth, Pastor of Faith Baptist Church, Kaiserslautern, Germany (an American military church – but it important to realize that the military is a sub-group of American culture in many ways, and that the spouses of American military also represent a very diverse international group)
- Jeff Hinman, Pastor of International Baptist Church, Duesseldorf, Germany
- Rodrigo Assis da Silva, Pastor of Bethel International Baptist Church, Frankfurt am Main, Germany

- William Colledge, Pastor of International Baptist Church of Zuerich, Switzerland
- Doug Beyer, Emirates Baptist Church International, Dubai, United Arab Emirates – Doug has served as interim pastor in seven different international churches around the world.
- Lyle Watson, Pastor of Tamarindo International Church, Guanacaste, Costa Rica
- Scott Carter, Founding Pastor of International Church at Mont Kiara, Kuala Lumpur, Malaysia
- Gerhard Venter, Pastor of International Baptist Church, Bratislava, Slovakia

They did not all respond to every question.

1. What experience do you believe was the most helpful to prepare you to pastor an international church?

Erik Nielsen: My upbringing in a multicultural home and my education in a multicultural, international school.

Scott Chadwick: We had the opportunity to spend nearly 3 months on the field on an interim basis in Sofia prior to coming back full-time. During that period we attended the ACM in Stuttgart and was introduced to the work of IBC. Very beneficial and instrumental in our return.

James Goforth: Growing up in a home that valued people from every group or background. My grandfather was a missionary to American Indians. My Father pastored a church that intentionally reached into communities that were not liked and in greatest need.

Jeff Hinman: I have lived overseas before pastoring an International Church. I spent time as a child overseas and I was in the Peace Corps as a young adult. This allowed me to not expect the International Church to not be like an "American" church.

Rodrigo Assis da Silva: Being born and brought up in a multicultural country (Brazil) helped a lot. Being a missionary to Africa and Wales before going into pastorate also helped. But the most helpful experience for me was the opportunity of being an assistant pastor of a multicultural international church before becoming the lead pastor of one.

William Colledge: To a small degree, my attendance at a few International Conferences over the years gave me some insight into the diversity in the international Christian community as did a brief preaching tour in Germany and Holland a few years before taking my first call to an International Church; but nothing significant really prepares one for such a unique ministry.

Doug Beyer: Though I didn't know it at the time, hosting a foreign exchange student in our home was teaching me to speak more slowly and with good diction. When communicating with those who speak English as a second language you'll teach twice as much if you speak half as fast.

Lyle Watson: I'm a military kid, grew up in my childhood years in the Philippines. I think this made cultural assimilation easier regarding the Latino culture.

Scott Carter: Serving as a youth pastor in an int'l church previously. Seeking the wisdom of other international church leaders.

Gerhard Venter: Living and ministering in a multi-cultural country, South Africa, as well as participating in several short-term mission trips around the world.

2. What was the most helpful advice you received to help you pastor an international church?

Erik Nielsen: My mentor pastor, when I began in Copenhagen, told me how the church used to cope with the interim pastors that led the congregation six to eight months at a time: "If we didn't like him, the rest of us agreed, 'well, we only have to make it through a few months, so let's just make the best of them.' And, if we did like him, we agreed, 'we only have a few months with him, so let's make the best of them.'" Our international church has such transient people, so I often think of those words when we have people who may be difficult to get along with.

Scott Chadwick: Hearing from IBC pastors/leaders about the transitory nature of an international/expat church really helped us prepare for the reality of it. Now that we've been here for 4 years we fully know the "pastoring a parade", "pastoring a circus" clichés well.

James Goforth: As a Pastor in general, as a church plant pastor I was once told "If you do everything the Lord tells you to do and the church closes / fails, YOU are not a failure" ... It helped me have a mindset that Obedience is Success' only measurement.

Jeff Hinman: If you found pleasing everyone in the US church hard, it is impossible in an International Church with so many different cultures and expectations. So just keep your eyes on Christ.

Rodrigo Assis da Silva: Listen to people, spend time with them, show interest to learn about their cultural backgrounds and the way they view God and church, appreciate them for whom they are.

William Colledge: It was the advice from a Christian businessman who was familiar with the particular mindset in my current ministry that has proved most helpful and that was to not be in a hurry to introduce changes to soon, the message that this could convey is that the "old way" isn't good enough, but rather to affirm that which is taking place before winning the leadership over to possible alternatives for the good of the ministry.

Doug Beyer: The preceding pastor of the Union Church of Manila (my first International Church) taught me to work hard to maintain English as the only language used in worship. In an International Church it is the only language that includes everyone. To speak Tagalog excludes those who haven't learned it yet. English is the only International Language and must be used in International Churches. Bi-lingual locals are often the majority in many International

Churches, but they are there because they want to worship in English. They do forget, however, that when they speak to each other in the local language they unintentionally exclude others who only speak English.

Scott Carter: "If this is what the Lord is leading you to do, you need to do it. Don't let anyone stop you (including existing mission board strategy)."

Gerhard Venter: Expect difficulties in adjusting (culture shock). Use simple English to accommodate non-English speakers.

3. What did you wish someone had told you before you arrived on the field?

Erik Nielsen: I wish someone would have assured me that when people choose not to follow Biblical counsel, they are rejecting the Lord, not His messenger. I often feel like I have failed in the delivery of the message.

Scott Chadwick: That our family would feel forsaken by us back in the States and that we would have to prepare for this in some way, rather than getting here and trying to work it out from this side of the pond. We hear this from other missionaries as-well. I would have liked to have fully known the details of the conflict between my predecessor and the deacons that occurred between the time we left and returned. This was never fully dealt with and now none of those in the middle of it are here. (The good news is everything is settled now, but there was a period of two years of awkwardness).

Jeff Hinman: You need to be clear as to what your 4 or 5 core values are and why you hold them because they will be challenged in an International Church. Expect conflict and decide before you are in the midst of the fight where you will not move and where you will. It is too exhausting to try and figure all this out on the fly.

William Colledge: "Don`t expect everyone to embrace your style of ministry immediately that you bring from your home country, as effective as you may have felt it was in that context!"

Scott Carter: Well, I was already on the field, but shifted into this role of planting and pastoring this new church. I do wish I had a greater understanding not just in cross-cultural leadership, but leading a multi-ethnic group. Granted this is a rather small, niche need. There are more resources out there now. I wish I had had a greater understanding of pastoring, making the shift from missionary to pastor.

Gerhard Venter: The challenges of finding your way around a new culture, e.g. totally foreign language, medical "systems" that work very different to my home country.

4. What is the greatest joy you have received as an international church pastor?

Erik Nielsen: To have friends with whom I can be friend as well as a pastor. The time with most people in an international church usually is so brief that people treat you only as their pastor.

Scott Chadwick: The beauty in the diversity of our congregation and that both rich and poor attend and contribute to the ministry brings me great joy.

James Goforth: Impacting a broad base and ever enlarging base of heroes who will spread the message of freedom all over the world.

Jeff Hinman: I have experienced more people coming to Christ in an International Church than in the US. When the truth of the gospel is shared is seems to have a greater impact.

Rodrigo Assis da Silva: The personal enrichment and encouragement that comes from being around people from so many nations and learning from them and their experiences. Every day my vision and perception of God and His love is broadened, just by being here among them.

William Colledge: Enjoying the diversity of cultural groups, denominational backgrounds and the willingness for many to "come on board!"

Doug Beyer: Baptizing eight new believers from four different countries in the Persian Gulf at the Easter Sunrise Service.

Scott Carter: Having a front row seat in seeing the Lord bring together people from all over world, into one local church. It truly is a foretaste of heaven, as we read in Revelation 7:9. Seeing people various ethnicities come to faith in Christ and baptize them. Seeing men grow in their faith and leading their families and using their jobs and resources for the Kingdom.

Gerhard Venter: Love and acceptance by the members, all part of a new family in Christ – it's like home away from home.

5. What is the greatest challenge you faced as an international church pastor?

Erik Nielsen: To have to ask a key leader in the church to step down from their position. We had simply not been a careful enough judge of maturity and readiness.

Scott Chadwick: The various belief systems of our people from a wide-range of denominations. Everything from Orthodox, Catholic, Protestant traditions to the atheist and agnostics who attend which is due in large part to the 45 years of communism. We are also inundated with prosperity theology adherents and many who lean towards charismatic teachings. Additionally, we encounter practicing and non-practicing Muslims routinely. As a lifelong Baptist this is a great challenge but also a great opportunity for teaching doctrine.

James Goforth: Constant turnover.

Jeff Hinman: The constant need to quickly find and develop leadership because of rapid turnover is difficult.

Rodrigo Assis da Silva: Encouraging healthy, clear and effective communication – while people from some cultures are very direct, people from other cultures have to tell anecdotes to make a point. While nodding when someone is speaking is accepted by people from some cultures, it is not accepted by others. It takes time to learn all these differences and it takes a lot of effort to foster an environment where people don't have to be on guard all the time, but can relax and learn to put themselves in someone else's shoes.

Doug Beyer: Living in a foreign country makes most activities more complicated and time-consuming. You must learn the virtue of patience or you'll go crazy.

Lyle Watson: At the church I was pastoring prior to planting the church we are now in, there was very minimal qualified spiritual leadership of the church. In an international, English speaking setting I've found it hard to find good elders/leaders in the church. One way to approach this is the "work with what God has given you" approach, which didn't go so well in my experience. There is huge risk in leading a church with poorly qualified spiritual leadership. I believe this is an inherent risk in pastoring international churches because you may not have many mature, English speaking Christians in your international setting. Fortunately, as we have planted the church I am in now we were blessed with two couples who had recently moved to our area and who had church leadership backgrounds. If either of these two couples were ever to leave we would have a void of good mature leaders. I am now currently trying to raise up future leaders.

Scott Carter: Leading the multi-ethnic group that God brought together. While it's beautiful to see the various nations come together, these differences also bring baggage, both culturally and any Christian background they may have. Seeking unity within such diversity is difficult.

Gerhard Venter: Different cultures have different views of and expectations of me as a pastor. How am I to fulfill these expectations?

6. Have you had to shepherd the church through a transition? Describe that experience.

Erik Nielsen: The church seems to always be in transition with new people and new challenges. Shepherding the church has meant keeping people aware of the mission and vision of the church again and again. Thankfully, the transitions have mainly been those of growth-related change.

Scott Chadwick: When we were in Sofia for three months. Ray and Charlene Smith were in the USA. Sandy and I led them and ministered full time, we were involved in their Bible studies as-well-as learning from the missionary community.

James Goforth: Transition is constant because we lose one third of our church annually.

Jeff Hinman: Every year is a transition year. In the summertime at least a third of the current leadership leaves due to assignment changes. Sometimes it is half or more that move on. This requires a constant process of vision casting, leadership development, and reminding people about the mission of the church.

Rodrigo Assis da Silva: In my previous church, I had influenced the make-up of the leadership team to reflect the make-up of the church. Although people from African or Caribbean nations were over 70% of the church, they had little to no representation in the leadership team. It was a process of delegating and allowing them to exercise their gifts more publicly (teaching adult Sunday school classes, for instance) so that people would see the potential of some of them to take ministry team leadership roles.

William Colledge: Understanding the mindset of the local people which has greatly impacted even on those foreigners who had been here for some time, and not to attempt to convince them that your thinking is more beneficial, even if you believe that it may be!

Doug Beyer: I have served as Interim Pastor of seven International

Churches in six different countries. Each one was in transition. Working with the pastoral search committee I have learned to build bridges between what was to what will be.

Lyle Watson: We are planting the church I currently serve in. So I am pastoring the church from non-existence to existence. This is has been a real blessing, seeing the way God has moved to allow our church to come to life. We are only two and a half years into it, but excited to see our town have a church and to be a Christian presence in the community for the expats.

Scott Carter: Yes, I led the initiative to transition from me as planter/pastor to calling the first full-time pastor. This was at the request of a couple of the Elders. They wanted me to have a strong voice in the calling of the first pastor. This gave me a chance to seek continuity in doctrine, teaching, and leadership as the church moves into its next stage of development and growth.

Gerhard Venter: Previously the church had a bad experience with some of its leadership. The church is at a next "growth point" where we soon would need a larger place to meet. Both of these points above require wisdom, prayer, gentle leadership.

7. **What do you believe your church will be like twenty years in the future?**

Erik Nielsen: I believe the church will grow in size enough to support one or two new church plants around the city and possibly in another city in Denmark.

Scott Chadwick: The history of Sofia has been largely unchanged over twenty-two years. There is a relatively small expat community for the size of the city of nearly three million. I can see change occurring in the nationals through young families. I can see exponential growth of the Bulgarian people in twenty years but this is a slow process. Depending on world events, the refugee situation will ebb and flow. This has changed greatly in four years. I think the church will be very similar to now but with additional people. There is potential for the church to grow.

James Goforth: If the community stays relatively the same, the church will in many ways stay the same, but prayerfully continue to grow in number, and grow in diversity, while learning to reach the international community as well.

Jeff Hinman: I have no idea. We seem to be growing, but with the constant turnover and changing politics of the EU I expect that the church will always be in flux. We have the understanding that the International Church is one which equips people while they are with us to better serve in the Kingdom of God wherever they go next. In this way the influence of an International Church is greater than size might indicate.

Rodrigo Assis da Silva: Bethel IBC will continue to be a place that makes every possible effort to welcome people from every nation, teaching them the truth of the gospel and encouraging them in their walk with God. We will continue to be a church that is interested in better serve and be even better connected with the international community around us, not just on Sundays: having a better space to offer shelter for asylum seekers, offering German classes even more often than 4 times a week, establishing our Parents & Toddlers Group, etc.

William Colledge: In a way, soon after we landed, the time seemed right (as encouraged by the current leadership team) to embark on a Vision process, a journey which has proved most beneficial for the ministry and has created a wonderful sense of ownership and "buy-in" from many.

Lyle Watson: I believe our church will grow, have its own property, and making an impact not only among the expat population, but also among the nationals. I see our church hosting Spanish speaking services as well as English. I see more multicultural representation in our leadership. I believe our area is in its baby stages as a community, and twenty years from now it will be much more populated and active. I foresee our church "growing up" with our surrounding community over these years.

Scott Carter: International Church at Mont Kiara has the opportunity to grow much larger and plant other congregations in the area and in the region. I believe IC@MK can and will be a standout church in its doctrine and teaching (amidst such a pluralistic culture and even a confused Christian culture), and be a missional church engaging Kuala Lumpur, Malaysia and SE Asia. It will be a mother church birthing other churches.

Gerhard Venter: A thriving international community of believers, actively reaching out to expats in multiple ways, while at the same time being an influence in the local community, city, country.

8. What are the most effective things you have done as a church to grow the church and build unity?

Erik Nielsen: We have made involvement in ministry as accessible as possible so that even short-termers have a place to serve. We have also made the leadership board (Church Council) more accessible by distinguishing the role pastors and elders have on the Council and the role of ministry team coordinators on the Council. People who have not served in certain ministries, or on church boards, prior to their time at our church have discovered their own capabilities and the church has been better for it.

Scott Chadwick: We major on meeting the needs of others and bringing the whole body into the process. We have a strong LifeGroup that meets weekly and the missionary community assists with refugee ministry. The unconditional love for one another has bonded us together. Also, hosting several mission teams has encouraged our people and hosting the IBC ACM has contributed to our people seeing a greater body of churches and this has encouraged them greatly.

James Goforth: Verbalize our need for each other, verbalize our unity in Christ, Open our eyes to the monolith among us and need to be more Technicolor.

Jeff Hinman: There is a hunger for solid Biblical teaching. This is lacking in Europe so I have found it to be well received. Also sin which causes disunity, particularly gossip and complaining seems to be more prevalent in my experience, so this has to be confronted quickly and firmly.

Rodrigo Assis da Silva: First of all, our leadership team really reflects the church make up. That helps a lot to promote unity. Preaching on unity is also done quite often. Apart from that, our church has intentionally kept a strong focus on fellowship, encouraging people to take part on home groups, having regular bring & share meals at the church, etc. But one of the most effective things we do is to organise a special International Evening when people are encouraged to bring food from their own countries and do a short presentation (talk, singing, dancing, video, poem, etc.) to show a little bit of their culture. It is fun, it is informative, it helps people to feel valued and appreciated while helping everyone to have a taste of different cultures.

William Colledge: Better, closer to achieving the goals that have been set, many new converts and more matured disciples.

Doug Beyer: I preach sermons crafted to meet their interests and needs. I meet with the Pastoral Search Committee to help them in the search process, but am careful not to interfere with the decision of who they select as the next pastor. I reach out to all the different ethnic groups in the church to make them feel included in the Body.

Lyle Watson: Planting the church with our team, children's programs to reach families, mission trips serving the poor, relational ministry over time.

Scott Carter: Utilizing different languages and cultural aspects in our services and programs. Celebrating one another's cultures and languages. Persistent, continual, constant modeling of unity among different ethnicities in my own (family) life. Preaching the Gospel continually. The Gospel of Jesus Christ unifies us.

Gerhard Venter: Preaching the Word. Creating a family, loving, accepting atmosphere, where "strangers" in the country can find and worship God.

9. What would you do differently?

Scott Chadwick: Our evangelism and outreach ministry is almost non-existent. This is a priority that must be addressed with our new leadership team. I am doing my part in the work of an evangelist but getting the church engaged is the problem. The good news is we have leaders who are willing to learn and multiply themselves. The challenge will be moving it forward.

Jeff Hinman: I was too quick to fill leadership positions, particularly elder positions, when I first arrived. This turned out badly. I would be more patient to get to know people better before trying to move the church forward in organization and mission. Even though the turnover is rapid, you need to take the long view for yourself.

Rodrigo Assis da Silva: To start with, I would definitely read more about other people's experiences in serving at international multi-ethnic churches.

William Colledge: Again, giving clarity of direction with a renewed Vision and Mission for the ministry, connecting directly in visitation, caring in times of need etc. Another very practical event that created a strong sense of unity was a Spring-Cleaning Day, with a wonderful response as folk just arrived in droves to help clean the place up!

Lyle Watson: Be more patient in bringing people onto volunteer roles. We are a very transient church and there is a lot of come and go of volunteers. Sometimes we get some with personal agendas that rub against the grain of our church's vision. Getting them plugged in too soon can make for awkward exits from the church should it come to that.

Scott Carter: Two things for me here: a) I would view my team of Elders as my first concentric circle for discipleship. I would invest heavily in the spiritual lives of the Elders. b) Invest more heavily in the core group start up team. We did a good job of building the relationships, getting to know one another, praying together, but I would treat this group as my first small group.

10. What one piece of advice would you like to share with other pastors of international churches?

Erik Nielsen: Remember that international church ministry is a Kingdom effort and not just a local church effort. When you disciple, train and equip people who must subsequently travel onward or return to their home, it is not a loss but a win.

Scott Chadwick: We, as pastors, tend to focus on the people we are most like and who are like us, but we miss out on opportunities to minister to the nations when we do this. My advice is to routinely reach out to all groups in the congregation and learn their culture. We do this by hosting different people groups in our home to share a meal and learn. We intentionally do this and the result has been a real bond between people groups. We have noticed that our people will invite others to these events who are otherwise not connected to the church or even the faith. (We have encountered many Muslims who we count as friends and consider them to be seekers, they just don't know they're seeking Jesus yet).

James Goforth: Maximize your strengths, Be comfortable being who you are, while being Uncomfortable being anything other than what God has called you to be.

Jeff Hinman: The International Church is a miracle in that it survives at all given the dozens of countries, cultures and religious backgrounds all present under one roof. Do not take anything for granted. What is a "no brainer" for you as a pastor may very difficult for some people to accept. A good example is the practice of believer's baptism. So many come from a tradition with infant baptism which is far more than just an age issue – it is a theological issue concerning their understanding of salvation, their understanding of the church, their understanding of community, and their understanding of tradition which is not as easy to correct as simply pointing our scriptures relevant to the issue. So just understand this International "Baptist" Church is sometimes not very "Baptistic". Sometimes this is good, sometimes it is bad.

Rodrigo Assis da Silva: Spend time with people, talk to them, eat with them, show a genuine interest on them, their families and their cultural backgrounds. Even though we are pastors and have a lot to give, we have also lot to learn from them, their experiences, the ways they view God and church. The more we know about different cultures, the more prepared we are to minister to them. And the best way to learn is to spend time with them. In more practical terms, I would encourage pastors of international church to try to: make sure the leadership make up is not so different from the church make up; experiment with multi-lingual worship; invest time and money in simultaneous translation ministry; be extra careful not to be seen as having "favorites" in the congregation (inviting people home in a planned and organised way so that everyone gets invited, having a plan for giving gifts to everyone or no-one in the congregation for the occasion of birthdays and anniversaries, etc.)

William Colledge: Trust the Lord more than your own areas of strength and familiarity or experience in ministry, minister in humility with an open heart to learn from the people before endeavoring to teach them all your know!

Doug Beyer: Learn as much as you can about the history and personality of the church. If there has been, or is, controversy in the church withhold your opinions until you've heard from all sides. Use social media to connect with your members and prospective members. Facebook is a powerful tool to build community. If the church does not have an up-to-date master computer file of all members and visitors, make one. Email a weekly "Pastoral Epistle" to every interested person to inform and generate enthusiasm about the church.

Lyle Watson: Be sure not to be a lone ranger. Stay connected with other pastors.

Scott Carter: Find a mentor, someone with cross-cultural and multi-cultural leadership experience and lean heavily into their wisdom. Invest in discipling your leadership teams!

Gerhard Venter: Relax! Don't take yourself and the work you do too seriously. You will make mistakes, but if you love the people and they see that you are "genuine" or "real", they will love and accept you. Be flexible. Different cultures do things differently – they may even define or see sin(s) differently from what you are used to. Don't become legalistic, but share the Word of God in a loving, dynamic way.

CLOSING REFLECTIONS

There is an up-beatness from the pastors of international churches, and though we have honestly looked at the challenges, I would do a disservice to us all if I did not stress the overall positive sense of the Lord's work and blessing in these fellowships. This is the Lord's work and Christ is, as He has always done, building His church.

To me, as the editor of the material, one of the most obvious observations of this study is the uniqueness of each experience. In the international or multicultural church there are a wide range of backgrounds, cultural values, Christian experiences, *and these various backgrounds also translate into the experiences and perspectives of the pastors themselves.* To me it is a clear indication that it is Christ who builds His church, and what is advisable in one situation may not be advisable in all.

Not only are the people different from one another but each church is different, each pastor is different, and each experience of pastoring is different in some ways from other experiences. Of course, on some level this is true in every place, even among churches existing in mono-cultural settings. But it seems to be true on a much larger scale among international churches.

Yet there are some general observations that can be made in light of these different experiences.

Stressors in Pastoring

The number one and number two stressors that come into the lives and ministries of pastors of international churches are the reality of short term relationships and multicultural congregations. In the midst of these challenges the pastor and his family must constantly reinvent their support base – the friends, encouragers, supporters, and co-laborers who help us to keep going. The pastor must learn to minister effectively to people from different nationalities and very likely different denominations, and to find supportive friends from these same people.

Every person who has ever moved to another country knows the stress of adjustment. The short term adjustment we call "culture shock" is usually mostly done within the first six to ten months. But then the long-term adjustment can take a lifetime! Some people must learn new languages just to survive. All must learn new ways of doing things, new ways of seeing things, new ways of interacting with others. Directness and indirectness, personal privacy or a complete lack of personal privacy, prejudices, guilt and shame, risk and non-risk – all of these issues, and many, many more become challenges to deal with – in life and in church.

Just to consider that everyone in the church is experiencing some stress in these areas is sobering – the pastor and leadership team, and every family and individual in the church. To pastor under these situations is very much like a doctor treating others while he suffers from the same disease. So, it is not mere platitude to say that only by the grace of God are we able to hold up, exist, and move forward.

Leadership Challenges

Quite a number of pastors mentioned the challenges they have faced in dealing with immature church leadership.[101] Most pastors around

---

[101] It is important to point out that though the subject of ineffective leadership was mentioned, no individuals were named in this book.

the world could probably echo that same thought, yet international churches seem to be more vulnerable to this factor. Part of the issue is that when dealing with people from other cultures, we are often not able to interpret their experience, their habits, their personalities, and even their actions to make a fair and accurate assessment of their character. The "new" to us often seems "interesting" and "refreshing" when in reality it is just different. Any number of international church pastors will tell you about the initial enthusiastic naivety with which they embraced some people, only later to realize their true level of spiritual maturity, or lack of it.

And, of course, this is a two-way street. We may also be too strict and under-esteem someone's true spiritual condition due to things that are taboo for Christians to do in our own culture. Some cultures have a "tight" view of Christian morality, forbidding some activities and insisting on others, while other cultures have a "loose" view of Christian morality, insisting more on abstract values of patience and acceptance of others and sincerity in speech. Each culture has some lamentable weaknesses that the Christians in that culture just accept and don't think much about, but that may very well stand out to other cultures as revealing a lack of true maturity and character.

Establishing trust, and often re-establishing it, between the leadership of the church and the people is an essential thing to do. No church will exist in peace and harmony and effective ministry if the people lack confidence in the spiritual qualifications of their leadership. And when leadership must be removed, or leaves under less than positive conditions, it is traumatic to the church. The expectations of what church leadership will do, how they will exercise their responsibility and calling, will also vary from culture to culture, and one may be doing a splendid job in the mind of some, while others are not satisfied.

It is easy in the midst of change and multiculturalism to misread the spiritual maturity of someone, to naively give someone responsibility when they are not ready for that responsibility, and to unwittingly set the church up for problems. Speaking of ordination, the biblical command is to "lay hands on no man quickly" (1 Tim. 5:22), not "do not lay hands on any man at all." So this command still must be followed by personal observation rising out of our own personal experience into someone's level of maturity. It is very easy to make a mistake here.

As many of us have observed, the challenge of interpreting someone's maturity also leads to churches selecting pastoral leadership to choose unqualified individuals. Sometimes it is not just the "new" that confuses us; we may also select someone who reminds us of people from our home nation, even though they may not be spiritually qualified. For example, someone from a warm and embracive culture may be attracted to a pastoral candidate who acts friendly, who smiles and warmly greets people, even though he is spiritually unqualified for the position.

The Blessings of the Work

The overriding enthusiasm for the international church work is contagious. Every one of the pastors of international churches I have spoken to over the years – with only one notable exception – has been enthusiastic about the multicultural church and ministry. There is a clear consensus about this matter and I can speak for my colleagues when I say that we believe God is at work in today's world through the international churches. That does not mean they are always easy to pastor and lead – they are quite demanding – but there is something wonderful about them that is difficult to express.

Some have called them a taste of heaven – for we read in Revelation 7:9: "After this I looked, and there before me was a great multitude that no one could count, from every nation, tribe, people and language, standing before the throne and before the Lamb." However, it is not the international or multicultural throng alone that is special – we should remember that hell has the same ethnic diversity – rather it is the work of God within the international community, the fact that Christ is making His presence known in so many lives from so many different cultures.

Grasping the True Potential of the International Church

I was challenged, encouraged, and enlightened by each chapter and each comment from each pastor and writer. Jimmy, David, Harry, Larry, Bob, Jacob, and Michael, thank you each for your contributions. Each comment from the pastors has likewise helped me in some way, and I believe can help you also if you are pastoring an international church, or you are simply involved in one.

Jacob Bloemberg's chapter in particular challenges all of us connected with the international church to see our true God-given potential to touch a whole city for Christ. The multicultural church is particularly enabled by God to see the various parts of the city, and even of the world and to reach out where the local churches may be blind to the people and to the opportunity.

After reading Jacob's article, I had to ask myself if we at Stuttgart have even begun to consider our true potential. It is often said of leaders of democratic organizations that we should not get too far ahead of the people we lead, half a step is enough, because if we do we will seem to be unrealistic. As a long serving pastor I have experienced the reality that most people in the church have their own concerns to think about. They see the church as it ministers to them and to their family, and this is all very understandable. The church gains the support to reach others because of the investment and impact it makes in the lives of its present members and attendees.

One of the ongoing challenges of an international church is dealing with the constant turnover, which usually "cuts to the bone," that is, it also impacts the leadership team and the sense of vision and direction. Normally, whoever you start any project with, by the time you finish you will have a very different group of people involved in it. *It is hard to build a building to the heavens if someone keeps changing out the weight-bearing blocks at the bottom.* Every now and then someone comes into the church and wants to change everything, and then they are gone within a few months or a couple of years. The challenge a pastor of an international church is how to balance this enthusiasm, sense of excitement, and realistically bring it all into some type of reasonable "doable" and sustainable means.

Any redirection or reorganization of a church or any organization requires a period of time to adjust to the new shape of things. During this adjustment time effectiveness is at a minimum, because so much energy is spent on just adjusting and getting used to the new things, including terminology, relationships, leadership, and allocation of resources. So it is unwise to reorganize all of the time, even if the new organization would be a better one.

But the leaders of the church must have a vision from God, an idea of the true need of their city and of the true potential of their church. God has said that with Him all things are possible, so none of our churches needs to shy away from a challenge or underestimate their potential. We all have limitless potential under the Lordship of Christ. As servants of Christ we must call the people of God to a vision that is greater than ourselves, that takes into our hearts the needs of the world today, *and what is the next step.*

Some of the pastors responded to the question about leading the church through a transition, "We are always in a transition." I know too well the reality of this statement. This is one of the greatest challenges of leading an international church, trying to balance transitional people and long-term needs, and long-term opportunities of ministry. Constant transition does not mean, however, that we do not also need major transitions from time to time, in order to become the church He calls us to be. We must transition to be churches that by the Holy Spirit find a way to become all that we can become in Him.

I have learned over the years the meaning of the scripture, "by wisdom a house is built, through understanding it is established" (Prov 24:3). Acts 6:1-7 reveals how important wisdom was for the early church; they chose men filled with the Spirit and with wisdom. Leaders need to have the leadership of God's Spirit to lead and guide, but also good, godly wisdom about the decisions they make. It is one thing to have a great and long-term vision of what the work of God in one church can become, yet the journey will only be completed one step at a time. *The most important thing that the leaders of a church need to have is an understanding of what the next step for the church should be in its growth and in its Christ-following journey.*

The sense of vision and enthusiasm for the work is also contagious. The Lord is doing something in the international churches around the world. He is building His kingdom. Those of us who have served in them can tell you that it is not always easy, but the Lord is good and faithful to supply us with what we need. I am reminded of what Major Ian Thomas said of the Christian life: It is not easy to live the Christian life, but neither is it hard. It is impossible. I would say the same of pastoring an international church – we must depend on God's miraculous strength and guidance to serve effectively.

The Influence of Long-term Pastors

I loved Larry Jones' article as well, not only because Larry and I are old friends, but because it dealt with the heart of the matter of reaching people – grasping the love of God for each person. Growth and expansion happens as the people of God take the love of God for others upon their hearts, and move as the Spirit leads them. I should confess that I took the flags down when I came to the church, and we no longer have the regular parade of flags – they were faded and a bit worn – but the spirit of what he wrote we still abide by. There is more than one way to acknowledge each person's importance while focusing also on who draws us together, namely Jesus Christ.

And Larry's story also shows the impact a permanent pastor can make on a congregation. In the midst of constant change, the position of pastor is very important. Of course, God does lead people to different places to serve, sometimes very quickly, and personal family needs are factors as well to consider as well, so though all of these factors should be taken into consideration it can also be noted that the pastors who serve the longest make the greatest impact for

Christ. And this is true in international churches also!

The Right Values and Timing

Combining all of the articles, I believe the key to making a difference for Christ in the international church will be found not only in preaching the right message, singing the right songs, or running the right programs, but especially in having the right values, especially the value of love for others. This will, in the long run, be more effective in seeing changes in people and changes in our world.

The old axiom, "We go where we are celebrated, not where we are tolerated," has great significance for the international church. If we merely tolerate people of different nations and cultural backgrounds, then we cannot expect them to feel welcomed. Yet displays of diversity that alienate others and distract us from our God-given mission also need to be checked. There must be a balance established between accepting and even celebrating the diversity and different cultural backgrounds, and keeping our eyes on Christ as He molds us into one people. Our ultimate goal is not diversity but unity and oneness in Christ, and transformation into Christ-likeness.

As I already mentioned, hell has the same ethnic diversity as heaven. Our ultimate focus cannot be on diversity alone, or even on celebrating the different cultures among us – though we may recognize people from different backgrounds and affirm them as loved and valued. Our ultimate goal is to be Christ's people, to bring glory to God, to emphasize the values and culture of the kingdom of God, to let His kingdom predominate and determine who we should be. Diversity for the sake of diversity will grow old eventually, and people will withdraw into what is comfortable and less threatening to them.

One of the valid uses of cultural uniqueness is the precise phraseology of some Bible passages, the use of theological and Christian terms that mean something personal to people of different nations. In fact, often surprising insights into the truth of God comes when we consider another language's scriptural interpretation, or another culture's observation and celebration of the Christian faith. The Asian sense of community touches the Western individualistic perspective. The African emphasis on harmony is also helpful for the greater Christian community, and similar observations can be made about every nation and culture on the globe.

For example, a few weeks ago while preaching through the gospel of Matthew, I mentioned that the accusation against Jesus by the Pharisees, that He cast out demons by the power of Beelzebub the prince of demons (Matt. 12:24), though wrongly said against Jesus, was not unrealistic for the Canaanite culture around them. I went on to mention how many people people in the world will go to someone with so-called "spiritual power" – a witch doctor, a witch, a spiritist – and seek to get them to reverse a curse, calling on one demon to defeat another demon. It was interesting to see the reaction in the congregation; many from developing nations shook their heads in agreement. Christ said in this passage that both demons work for the same "strong man" – Satan himself.

An important pastoral trait in that type of setting is patient compassion, that understands the hold that this type of superstition can have on people, and consistently teaches and encourages people to a biblical position. To blatantly dismiss all of this as nonsense leads the people to assume that the pastor does not understand their weaknesses. The deceptions of Satan are lies, but they are powerful lies, and must be dealt with in the power of the Spirit. The divine authority we have in Christ to destroy strongholds (2 Cor. 10:4-5), is also to be exercised in the spirit of love, "speaking the truth in love" (Eph. 4:15).

The Supreme Value of Love

I do not believe that we can over-esteem the value of the divine love of Jesus in the church's life. "Love never fails" (1 Cor. 13:8) does not mean that it guarantees success in every instance of personal ministry – many have walked away from divine love – but that it never fails to truly love. The Corinthians were guilty of "preferring those things which are for a time to the graces which are for ever,"[102] namely, love, faith, and hope, but especially love. Though the main issues for the Corinthians were tongues and interpretation of tongues, Paul opened up the matter to the entire life and ministry of the church, about knowledge, prophecy, giving campaigns, organizational gifts, etc. Love, along with faith and hope, succeeds where all else fails.

Like many pastors I have sometimes heard people say, "What we should be doing is..." and it does not matter what the end of the sentence sounds like. We know that it will probably be unrealistic – driven by guilt, anger, or both, rather than led by the Spirit of God. What we should be doing is loving everybody and following the leadership of the Lord. Everybody, rich, poor, educated, common laborer, Asian, African, American, European, Latino, everyone is important to God. But we should also recognize that the Lord leads in this process, just as He frustrated the plans of Paul to reach out into the province of Asia, and redirected them to Macedonia (Acts 16:6-10). It is not only our hearts that must be prepared, but the people to whom we go must also be prepared by God, for Christ said, "No one can come to Me unless the Father who sent Me draws him" (John 6:44). He sent the disciples out with the command to look for the son of peace, and if they did not find him, then move to the next village until they did (Luke 10:5-12).

If our motive is the pure and abiding love of God, then we can expect Him to lead and guide us in the expression of love. We must seek to make sure we balance an adventurous spirit with a realistic assessment of our capacity to continue doing a certain ministry. A short termer may suggest and even actively serve in an area, but then in a few short months they are gone, and on the heels of their departure another short termer may arrive insisting that we do a different ministry entirely. So there has to be some divine common sense to our programming, along with divine endurance and patience. Divine leadership will show us what to do, and we should

---

[102] *Ellicott's Commentary*

distinguish between God's voice and human wills that stem more from guilt, an effort to recreate the familiar, or a desire to dominate and control others.

In my book *Look Who God Let into the Church* I confessed to a mistake I made in pastoring in Singapore – a mistake of the head, not of the heart. I had been taught and I had believed that the way to grow a church was through offering excellent programming. That, of course, is essential to do, but it is not enough by itself. What also needs to happen is for the people to feel that they are part of the same narrative, so building a common narrative, a common single history that all – short-termers and long-termers can identify with – is an essential element also in the health, unity, and vision of the church. Every culture relates to a story, and the church's story must be shared and told and felt as a story of unity and oneness – one with which each believer can in some way connect. Ultimately, after all, it is Christ who is building His church, and none other.

As for me, some of the best advice I have ever received in pastoring period is: Trust the Lord and trust the people. A pastor must learn faith in God and faith in God's work in His people. The apostle could say with confidence, "Being confident of this very thing, that he who has begun a good work in you will complete it until the day of Jesus Christ" (Phil. 1:6). Though we pastors must teach and challenge the people to grow, and though we will meet more than one immature believer along the way, as well as many unfit for leadership in the church, still we should not question the work of Christ in them. This is part of seeing each person as important, loved by God, with potential to follow Christ and mature in the faith.

It is my hope that this book will help further the work of God in multicultural churches, to sharpen their impact and to enrich their fellowship. And that we all might also find joy and fulfillment along the journey.

Made in the USA
Charleston, SC
26 February 2015